THE EASY WORSHIP FAKE BOOK

Melody, Lyrics and Simplified Chords

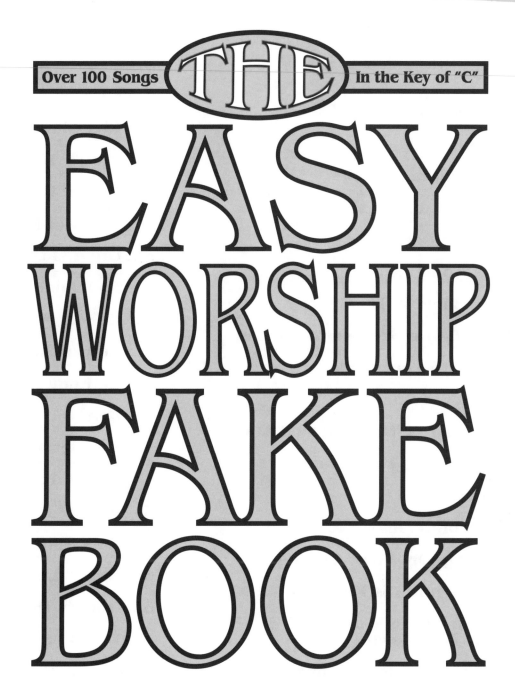

Over 100 Songs THE In the Key of "C"

EASY WORSHIP FAKE BOOK

ISBN 1-4234-0466-1

HAL•LEONARD®
CORPORATION

7777 W. BLUEMOUND RD. P.O. BOX 13819 MILWAUKEE, WI 53213

Visit Hal Leonard Online at
www.halleonard.com

THE EASY WORSHIP FAKE BOOK

CONTENTS

INTRODUCTION

What Is a Fake Book?

A fake book has one-line music notation consisting of melody, lyrics and chord symbols. This lead sheet format is a "musical shorthand" which is an invaluable resource for all musicians—hobbyists to professionals.

Here's how *The Easy Worship Fake Book* differs from most standard fake books:

- All songs are in the key of C.

- Many of the melodies have been simplified.

- Only five basic chord types are used—major, minor, seventh, diminished and augmented.

- The music notation is larger for ease of reading.

In the event that you haven't used chord symbols to create accompaniment, or your experience is limited, a chord speller chart is included at the back of the book to help you get started.

Have fun!

ALL HAIL KING JESUS

Words and Music by
DAVE MOODY

Majestically

All hail King Je - sus! All hail Em -

man - u - el:_____ King of kings, Lord of

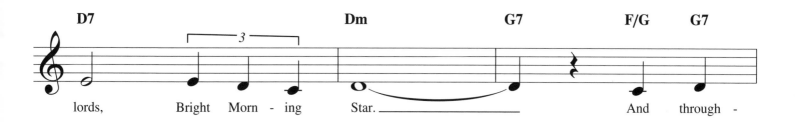

lords, Bright Morn - ing Star._____ And through -

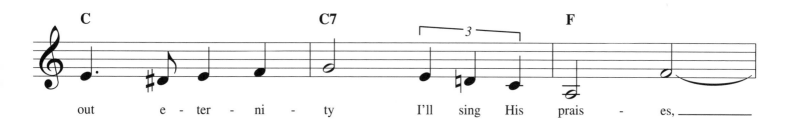

out e - ter - ni - ty I'll sing His prais - es,_____

_____ And I'll reign with Him through - out e - ter - ni - ty.

ABOVE ALL

Words and Music by PAUL BALOCHE
and LENNY LeBLANC

Worshipfully

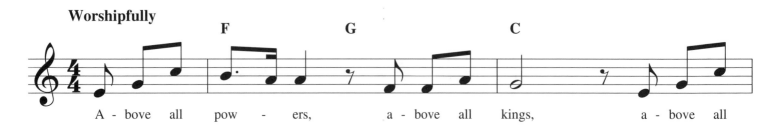

A - bove all pow - ers, a - bove all kings, a - bove all

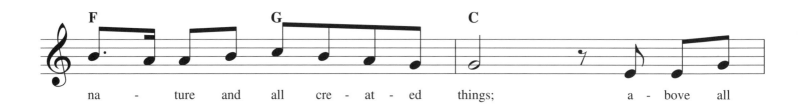

na - ture and all cre - at - ed things; a - bove all

wis - dom and all the ways __ of man, _____

You were here be - fore __ the world be - gan. A - bove all

king - doms, a - bove all thrones, a - bove all

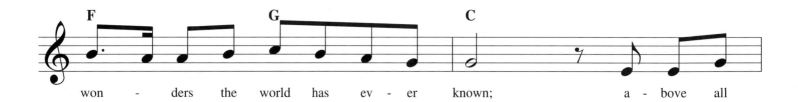

won - ders the world has ev - er known; a - bove all

wealth and treas - ures of ____ the earth, ____

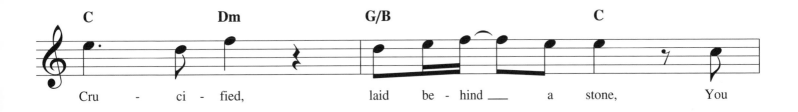

there's no way to meas - ure what You're worth.

Cru - ci - fied, laid be - hind ____ a stone, You

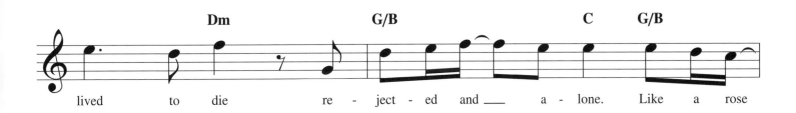

lived to die re - ject - ed and ____ a - lone. Like a rose

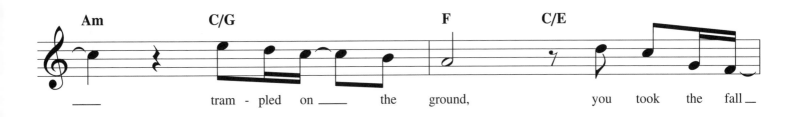

____ tram - pled on ____ the ground, you took the fall ____

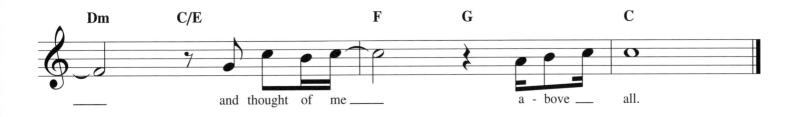

____ and thought of me ____ a - bove ____ all.

AGNUS DEI

Words and Music by
MICHAEL W. SMITH

Worshipfully

Al - le - lu - ia, _____

Al - le - lu - ia, _____ for the Lord God Al-might - y

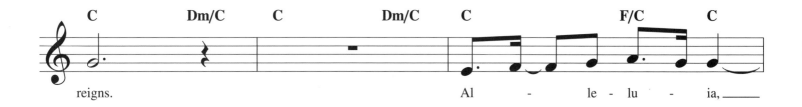

reigns. Al - le - lu - ia, _____

_____ Al - le - lu - ia, _____

_____ for the Lord God Al-might - y reigns.

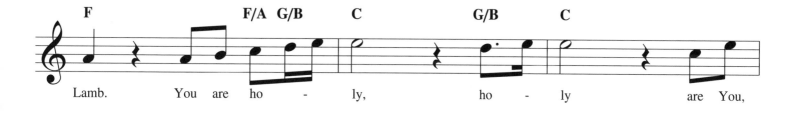

ANCIENT OF DAYS

Words and Music by GARY SADLER
and JAMIE HARVILL

Steady drive

Bless - ing____ and hon - or,   glo - ry____ and pow - er

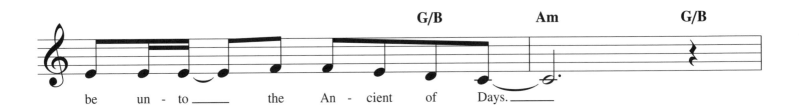

be un - to ____ the An - cient of Days. _____

From ev - 'ry na - tion,   all of ____ cre - a - tion,

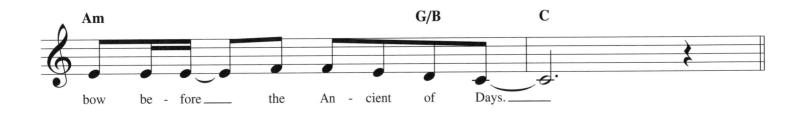

bow be - fore ____ the An - cient of Days. _____

Ev - 'ry tongue___ in heav - en and earth   shall de - clare ____ Your glo - ry.

Ev - 'ry knee___ shall bow at Your throne____   in wor - ship.

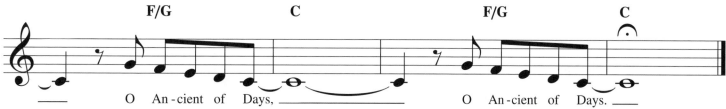

AS THE DEER

Words and Music by
MARTIN NYSTROM

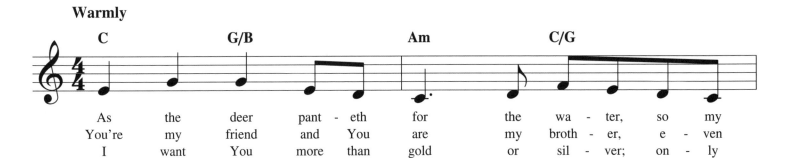

As   the   deer   pant - eth   for   the   wa - ter,   so   my
You're   my   friend   and   You   are   my   broth - er,   e - ven
I   want   You   more   than   gold   or   sil - ver;   on - ly

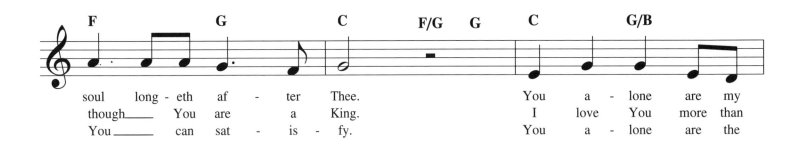

soul   long - eth   af - ter   Thee.   You   a - lone   are   my
though____   You   are   a   King.   I   love   You   more   than
You____   can   sat - is - fy.   You   a - lone   are   the

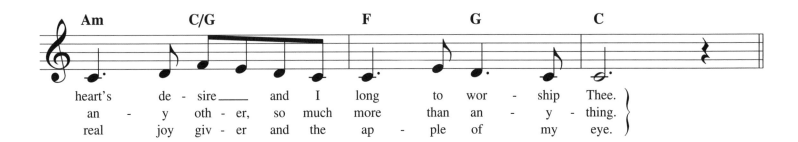

heart's   de - sire____   and   I   long   to   wor - ship   Thee.
an - y   oth - er,   so   much   more   than   an - y - thing.
real   joy   giv - er   and   the   ap - ple   of   my   eye.

You   a - lone   are   my   strength,   my   shield.   To   You   a - lone   may   my

spir - it   yield.   You   a - lone   are   my

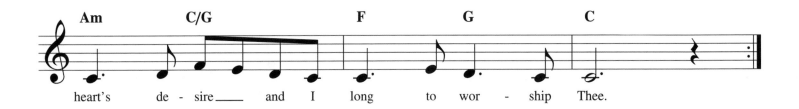

heart's   de - sire____   and   I   long   to   wor - ship   Thee.

AWESOME GOD

Words and Music by
RICH MULLINS

Strongly, in 2

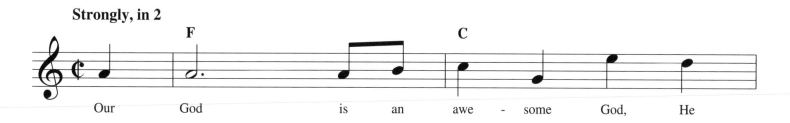

Our   God   is   an   awe - some   God,   He

reigns   from___ heav - en   a - bove   with___ wis - dom, ___

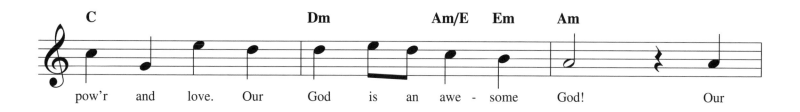

pow'r   and   love.   Our   God   is   an   awe - some   God!   Our

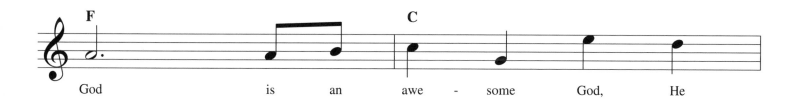

God   is   an   awe - some   God,   He

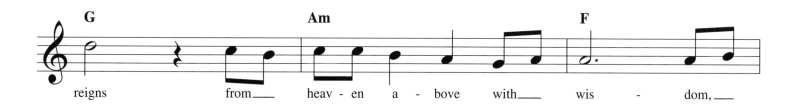

reigns   from___ heav - en   a - bove   with___ wis - dom, ___

pow'r   and   love.   Our   God   is   an   awe - some   God!

AWESOME IN THIS PLACE

Words and Music by
DAVID BILLINGTON

Moderately slow, in 2

As I come in-to＿＿ Your pres - ence, past the gates＿ of praise,＿

＿＿ in - to Your sanc - tu - ar - y, till we're

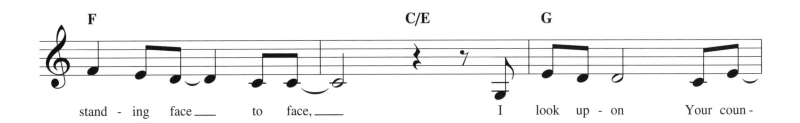

stand - ing face＿ to face,＿ I look up - on Your coun-

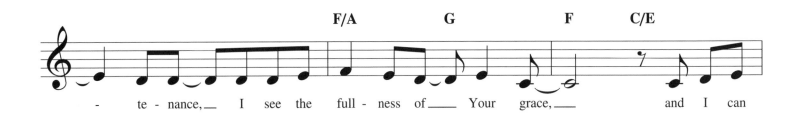

- te - nance,＿ I see the full - ness of＿ Your grace,＿ and I can

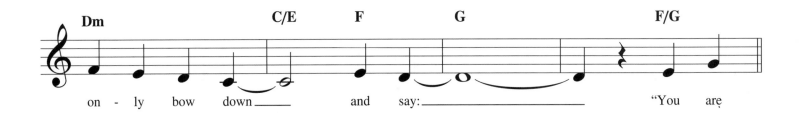

on - ly bow down＿ and say:＿＿＿＿＿ "You are

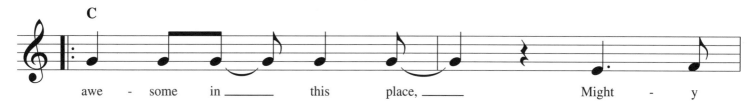

awe - some in _____ this place, _____ Might - y

God. _____ You are awe - some in _____ this place, _

_____ Ab - ba Fa - ther. _____ You are

wor - thy of _____ all praise, _____ to You our lives _____ we raise. _

_____ You are awe - some in _____ this place, _____ Might - y _____

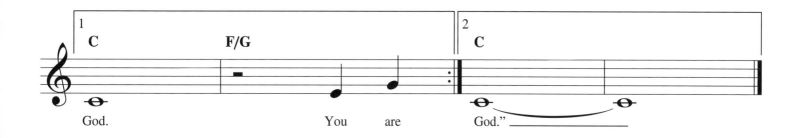

God. You are God." _____

BE UNTO YOUR NAME

Words and Music by LYNN DeSHAZO
and GARY SADLER

With motion, in one

We   are   a   mo -   ment,   You   are   for - ev -
We   are   the bro - ken,   You   are   the heal -

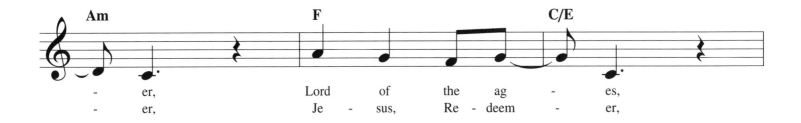

- er,   Lord   of   the   ag - es,
- er,   Je - sus,   Re - deem - er,

God   be - fore _____   time.   We   are   a   va -
might - y   to _____   save.   You   are   the   love _____

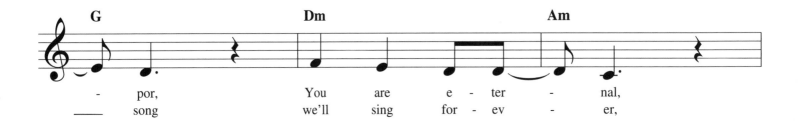

- por,   You   are   e - ter - nal,
_____   song   we'll   sing   for - ev - er,

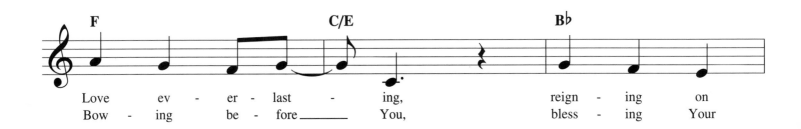

Love   ev - er - last - ing,   reign - ing   on
Bow - ing   be - fore _____   You,   bless - ing   Your

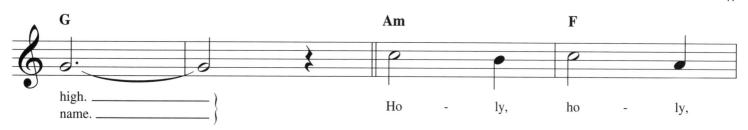

high. _____
name. _____

Ho - ly, ho - ly,

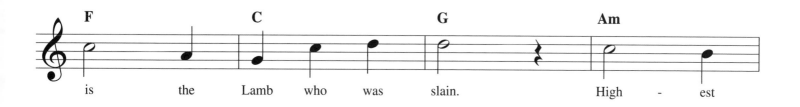

Lord God Al - might - y. Wor - thy

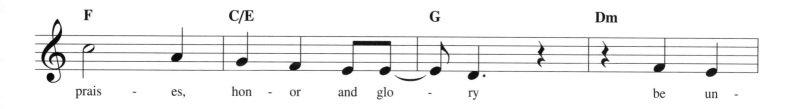

is the Lamb who was slain. High - est

prais - es, hon - or and glo - ry be un -

to Your name, _____ be un -

to Your name. _____

BETTER IS ONE DAY

Words and Music by
MATT REDMAN

Moderately, with a strong beat

How love-ly is Your dwell-ing place, O Lord Al-might-
thing I ask and I would seek: to see Your beau-

-y, for my soul longs and e-ven faints for
-ty, to find You in the place Your glo-ry

You. For here my heart is
dwells. One thing I ask and

sat-is-fied with-in Your pres-ence. I
I would seek: to see Your beau-ty, to

sing be-neath the shad-ow of Your wings.
find You in the place Your glo-ry dwells.

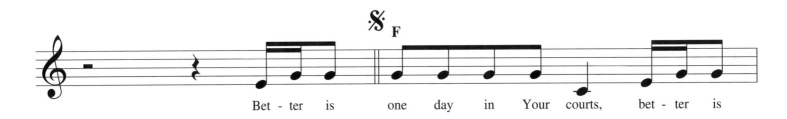

Bet-ter is one day in Your courts, bet-ter is

one day in Your house, bet - ter is one day in Your courts than thou - sands

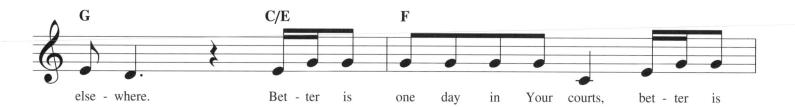

else - where. Bet - ter is one day in Your courts, bet - ter is

To Coda ⊕

one day in Your house, bet - ter is one day in Your courts than thou - sands

else - where, than thou - sands else - where. One

else - where. My heart and flesh cry out for You, the liv - ing God.

Your Spir - it's wa - ter to my soul. I've tast - ed and I've seen,

come once a - gain to me. I will draw near to You,

Dm **G**

I will draw near to You, _____ to You. _____

F **G** **F**

(Instrumental)

G **F**

Bet - ter is one day, _____ bet - ter is

G **C/E** **F** **F/A**

one day, _____ bet - ter is one day _____ than thou - sands

G **F**

else - where. Bet - ter is one day, _____ bet - ter is

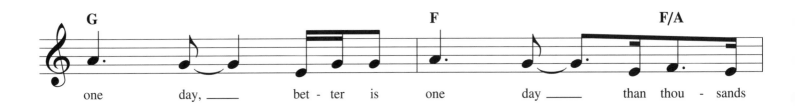

G **F** **F/A**

one day, _____ bet - ter is one day _____ than thou - sands

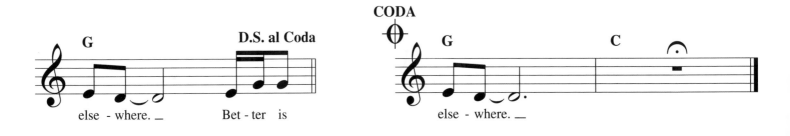

G **D.S. al Coda** **CODA** **G** **C**

else - where. _ Bet - ter is else - where. _

THE BATTLE BELONGS TO THE LORD

Words and Music by
JAMIE OWENS COLLINS

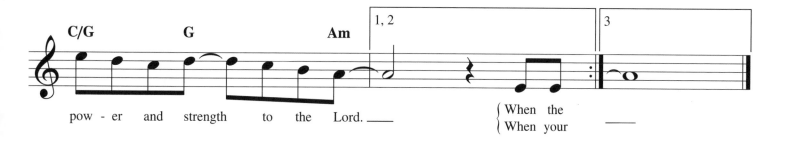

BLESSED BE THE LORD GOD ALMIGHTY

Words and Music by
BOB FITTS

Moderately

Fa - ther in heav - en, how we love You; we

lift Your name in all the earth. May Your

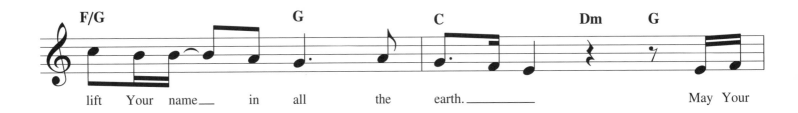

king - dom be es - tab - lished in our prais - es, as Your

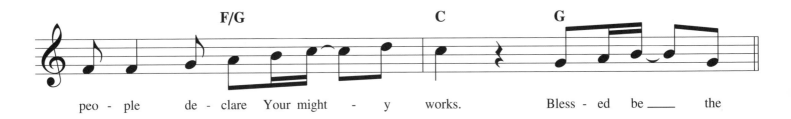

peo - ple de - clare Your might - y works. Bless - ed be the

Lord God Al - might - y, who was and is and is to

come. Bless - ed be the Lord God Al -

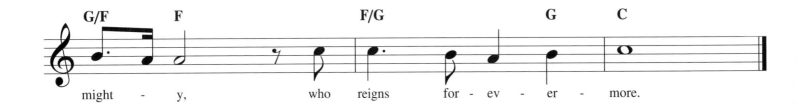

might - y, who reigns for - ev - er - more.

BREATHE

Words and Music by
MARIE BARNETT

With emotion

This is the air I breathe,   this is the
This is my dai - ly bread,   this is my

air I breathe,   Your ho - ly pres - ence   liv - ing in me.
dai - ly bread,   Your ver - y Word _____ spo - ken to me.

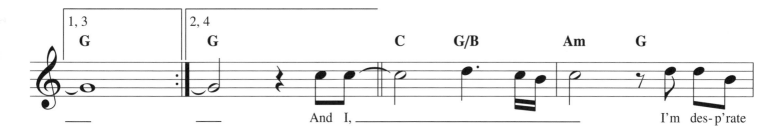

And I, _____ I'm des - p'rate

for You. _____ And I,

I'm lost with - out _____ You. _____

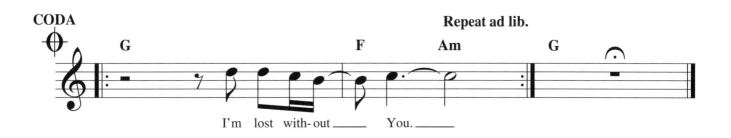

I'm lost with - out _____ You. _____

BLESSED BE YOUR NAME

Words and Music by MATT REDMAN
and BETH REDMAN

Rhythmically

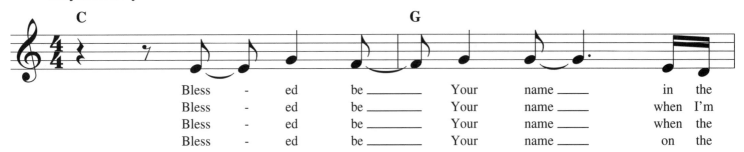

Bless - ed be _____ Your name _____ in the
Bless - ed be _____ Your name _____ when I'm
Bless - ed be _____ Your name _____ when the
Bless - ed be _____ Your name _____ on the

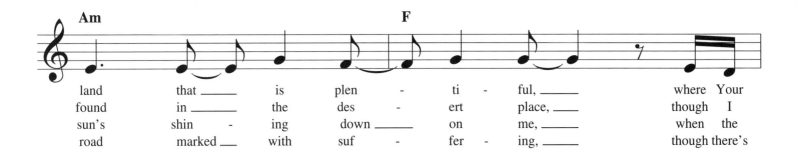

land that _____ is plen - ti - ful, _____ where Your
found in _____ the des - ert place, _____ though I
sun's shin - ing down _____ on me, _____ when the
road marked _____ with suf - fer - ing, _____ though there's

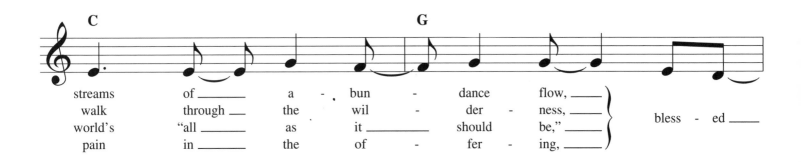

streams of _____ a - bun - dance flow, _____
walk through _____ the wil - der - ness, _____
world's "all _____ as it _____ should be," _____
pain in _____ the of - fer - ing, _____

bless - ed _____

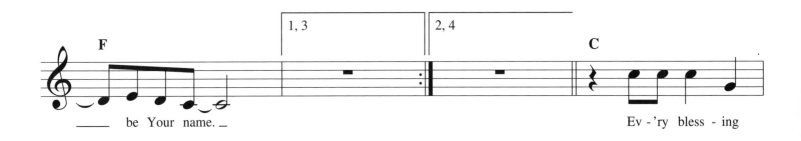

1, 3

2, 4

_____ be Your name. _

Ev - 'ry bless - ing

You pour out I'll turn back to praise.

When the dark - ness

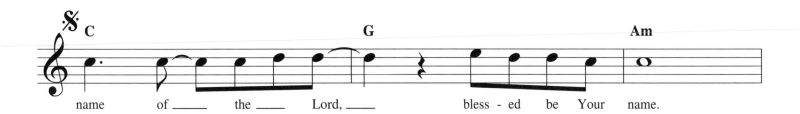

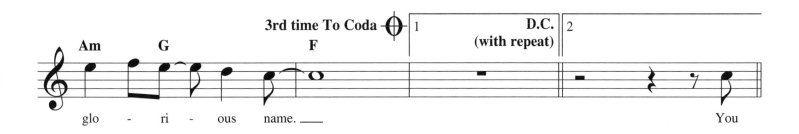

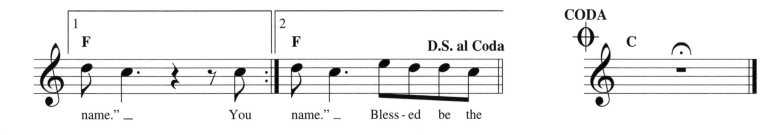

CELEBRATE JESUS

Words and Music by
GARY OLIVER

Driving

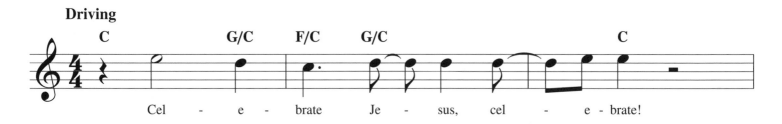

Cel - e - brate Je - sus, cel - e - brate!

(Instrumental) Cel - e - brate Je - sus, cel -

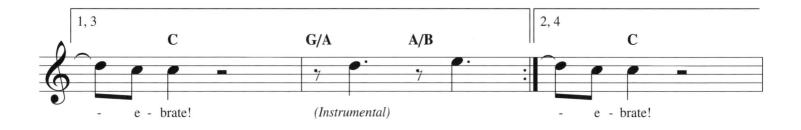

- e - brate! (Instrumental) - e - brate!

He is ris - en, _____ He is

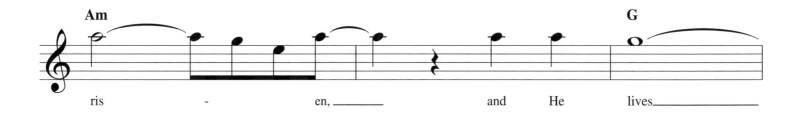

ris - en, _____ and He lives_____

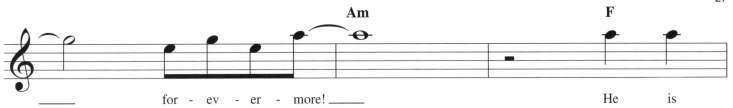

for - ev - er - more! _____ He is

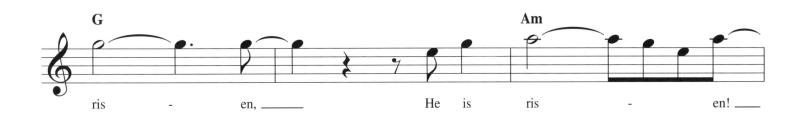

ris - en, _____ He is ris - en! _____

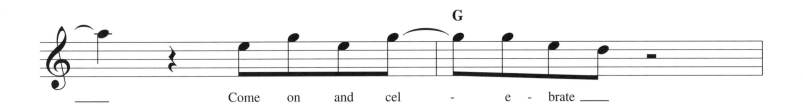

_____ Come on and cel - e - brate _____

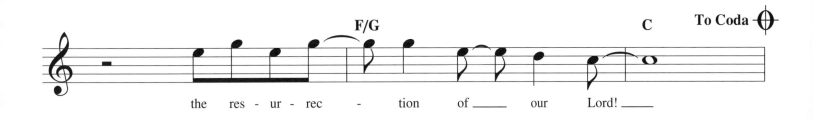

the res - ur - rec - tion of _____ our Lord! _____

D.C. al Coda (with repeat)

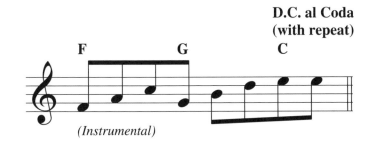

(Instrumental)

CODA

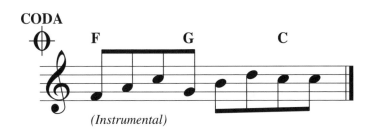

(Instrumental)

CHANGE MY HEART OH GOD

Words and Music by
EDDIE ESPINOSA

Prayerfully

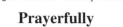

Change my heart, oh God, _____ make it ev - er true. _____

_____ Change my heart, oh God, _____ may I be like You. _____

You are the Pot - ter,

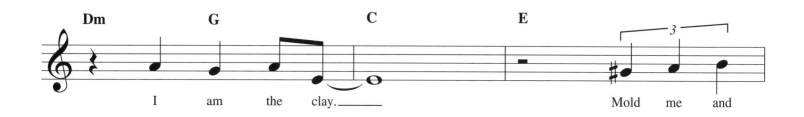

I am the clay. _____ Mold me and

make _____ me, this is what I pray.

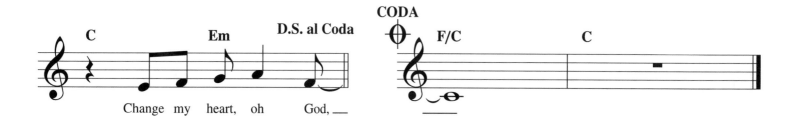

Change my heart, oh God, _____ _____

COME INTO HIS PRESENCE

Words and Music by
LYNN BAIRD

Joyfully

Come in-to His pres-ence with thanks-giv-ing in your heart and give Him

praise,_____ and give Him praise. Come in-to His pres-ence with thanks-

giv-ing in your heart, your voic-es raise,_____ your voic-es

raise. Give glo-ry and hon-or and

pow-er un-to Him,_____ Je-sus, the

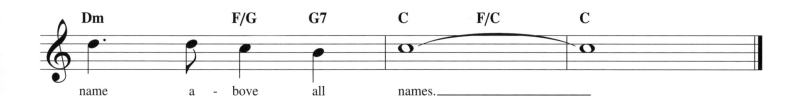

name a-bove all names._____

COME LET US WORSHIP AND BOW DOWN

Words and Music by
DAVE DOHERTY

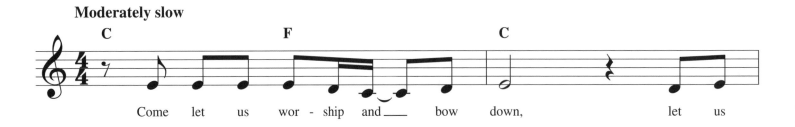

Come let us wor - ship and ___ bow down, let us

kneel be - fore the Lord, our God, our Mak - er.

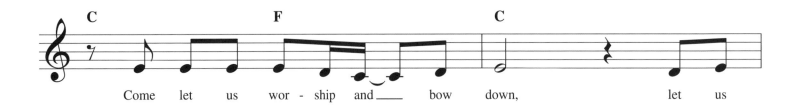

Come let us wor - ship and ___ bow down, let us

kneel be - fore the Lord, our God, our Mak - er. For He ___ is our

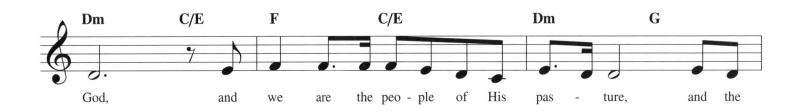

God, and we are the peo - ple of His pas - ture, and the

sheep ___ of His hand, just the sheep ___ of His hand.

COME, NOW IS THE TIME TO WORSHIP

Words and Music by
BRIAN DOERKSEN

Steady, driving

Come, now is the time to wor - ship.

Come, now is the time to give your heart.

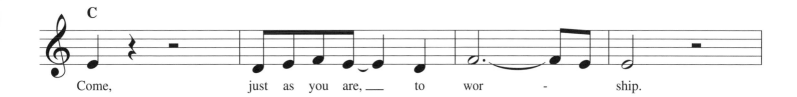

Come, just as you are, to wor - ship.

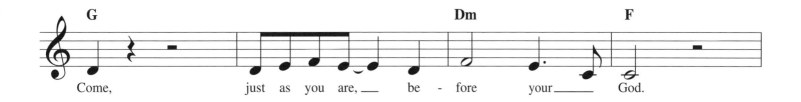

Come, just as you are, be - fore your God.

Come. One day ev - 'ry tongue will con - fess You are God,

one day ev - 'ry knee will bow. Still, the great - est treas - ure re - mains

for those who glad - ly choose You now.

CREATE IN ME A CLEAN HEART

Words and Music by
KEITH GREEN

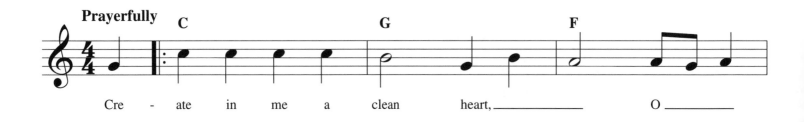

Cre - ate in me a clean heart, _____ O _____

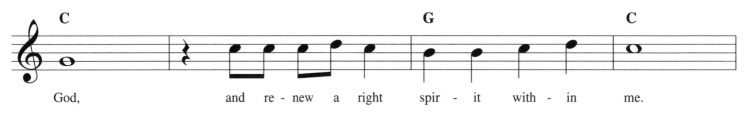

God,   and re - new a right spir - it with - in me.

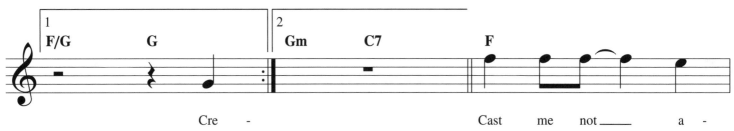

Cre -   Cast me not ____ a -

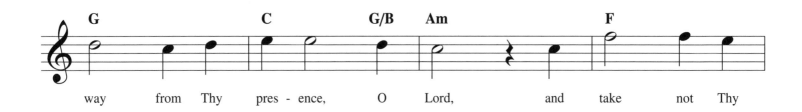

way   from Thy   pres - ence,   O   Lord,   and   take   not   Thy

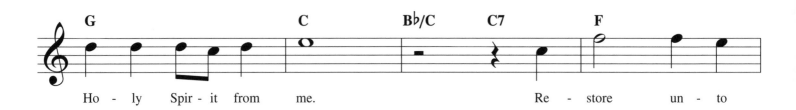

Ho - ly   Spir - it   from   me.   Re - store   un - to

me   the   joy   of   Thy   sal - va - tion,

and   re - new   a   right   spir - it   with - in   me. _____

CRY OF MY HEART

Words and Music by
TERRY BUTLER

DAYS OF ELIJAH

Words and Music by
ROBIN MARK

Steadily

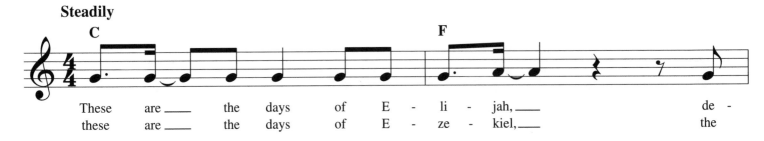

These are ___ the days of E - li - jah, ___ de -
these are ___ the days of E - ze - kiel, ___ the

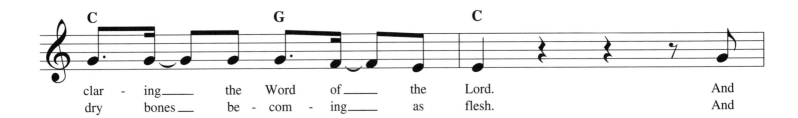

clar - ing ___ the Word of ___ the Lord. And
dry bones ___ be - com - ing ___ as flesh. And

these are ___ the days of Your ser - vant, Mo - ses,
these are ___ the days of Your ser - vant, Da - vid, re -

right - eous - ness be - ing ___ re - stored. And
build - ing ___ a tem - ple ___ of praise. And

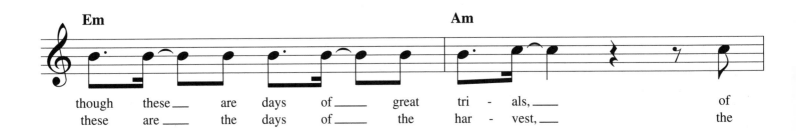

though these ___ are days of ___ great tri - als, ___ of
these are ___ the days of ___ the har - vest, ___ the

fam - ine ___ and dark - ness ___ and sword, still
fields are ___ as white in ___ the world. And

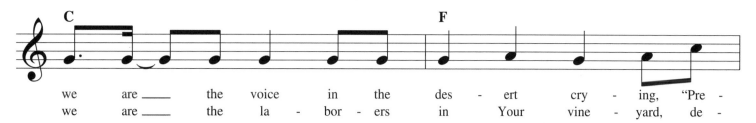

we are ____ the voice in the des - ert cry - ing, "Pre -
we are ____ the la - bor - ers in Your vine - yard, de -

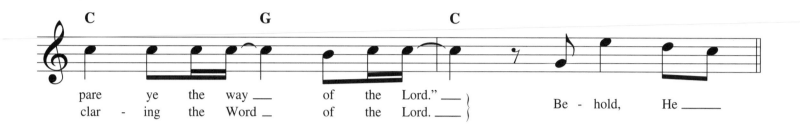

pare ye the way ___ of the Lord." ___ } Be - hold, He ____
clar - ing the Word _ of the Lord. ___ }

comes, rid - ing on the clouds, ___ shin - ing like the sun _

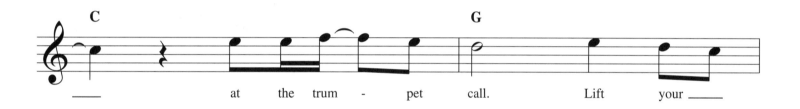

____ at the trum - pet call. Lift your ____

voice, it's the year of Ju - bi - lee ____ and out of Zi - on's

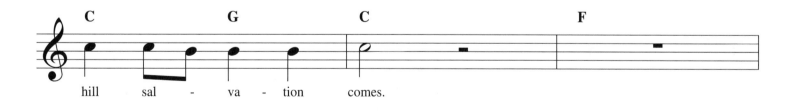

hill sal - va - tion comes.

And

There is no god like Je - ho - vah, there is no god like Je - ho - vah,

there is no god like Je - ho - vah, there is no god like Je - ho - vah.

There is no god like Je - ho - vah, there is no god like Je - ho - vah,

there is no god like Je - ho - vah, there is no god like Je - ho - vah.

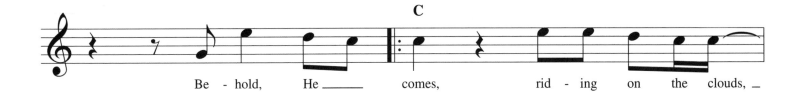

Be - hold, He _____ comes, rid - ing on the clouds, _

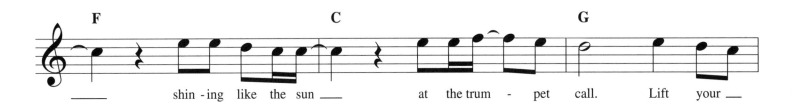

_____ shin - ing like the sun ___ at the trum - pet call. Lift your _

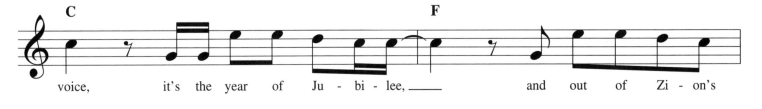

voice, it's the year of Ju - bi - lee, _____ and out of Zi - on's

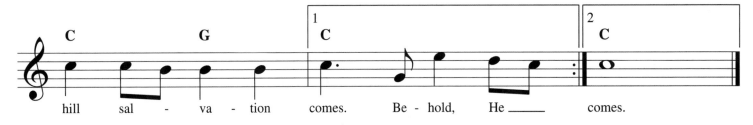

hill sal - va - tion comes. Be - hold, He _____ comes.

FIRM FOUNDATION

Words and Music by NANCY GORDON
and JAMIE HARVILL

Moderately fast

Je - sus, You're my firm foun - da - tion;___ I know I can stand___

___ se - cure.___ Je - sus, You're my firm foun - da - tion;___

I put my hope in Your ho - ly Word, _ I put my hope in Your ho -

- ly Word. ___

Last time Fine

I have ___ a liv - ing hope,
Your Word ___ is faith - ful,

(Echo:)

(I have ___ a liv - ing hope,) I have ___ a fu - ture.
(Your Word ___ is faith - ful,) might - y ___ in pow - er.

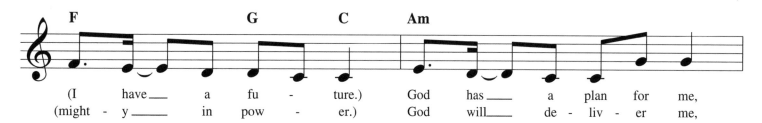

(I have ___ a fu - ture.) God has ___ a plan for me,
(might - y ___ in pow - er.) God will ___ de - liv - er me,

(God has ___ a plan for me,) of this I'm sure, ___ of this I'm sure! ___
(God will ___ de - liv - er me,) of this I'm sure, ___ of this I'm sure! ___

DRAW ME CLOSE

Words and Music by
KELLY CARPENTER

Draw me close _ to You, _____ nev - er let _ me go. _

_____ I lay it all _ down _ a - gain _

to hear You say _ that I'm _____ Your friend. _

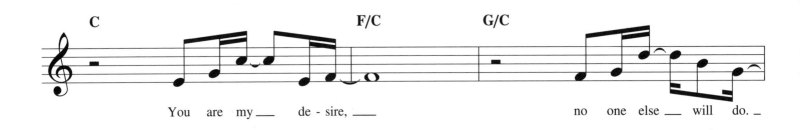

You are my _ de - sire, _ no one else _ will do. _

_ 'Cause noth - ing else _ could take _ Your place _

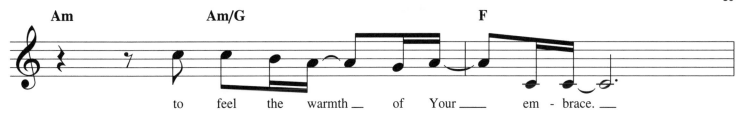

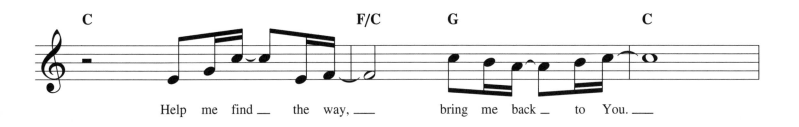

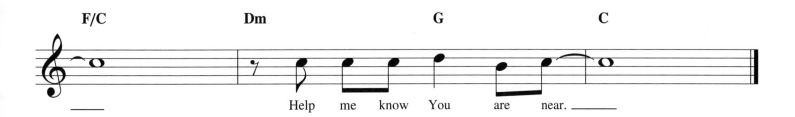

EAGLE'S WINGS

Words and Music by
REUBEN MORGAN

Moderately

Here I am wait - ing;_____ a - bide in me,___ I pray.___

____ Here I am long - ing for You._

_____ Hide me in Your___ love,_____

bring me to ____ my knees.____ May I know Je -

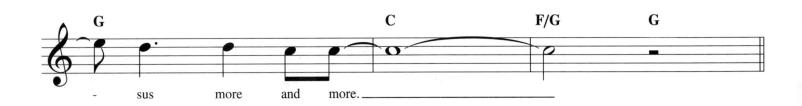

- sus more and more._____

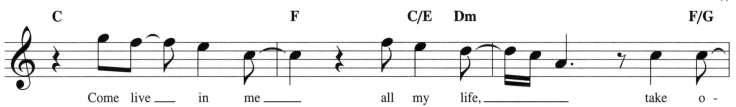

Come live ___ in me ___ all my life, _____ take o-

- ver. _____ Come breathe _ in me, _____ I will rise _

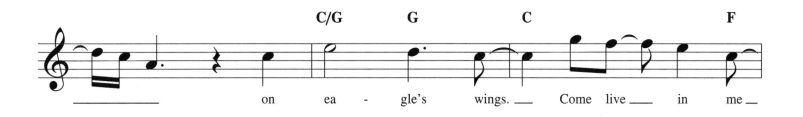

_____ on ea - gle's wings. ___ Come live ___ in me __

___ all my life, _____ take o - ver. _____

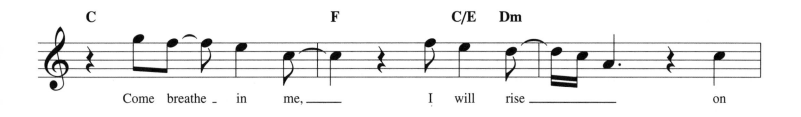

Come breathe _ in me, _____ I will rise _____ on

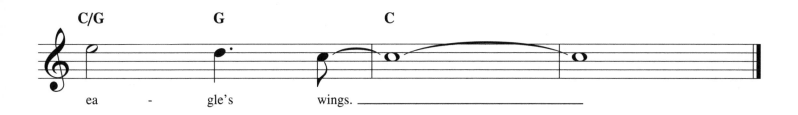

ea - gle's wings. _____

EVERY MOVE I MAKE

Words and Music by
DAVID RUIS

Moderately, in 2

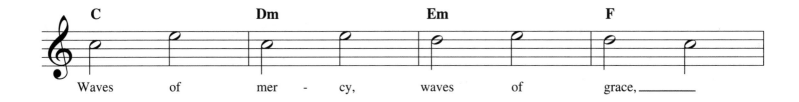

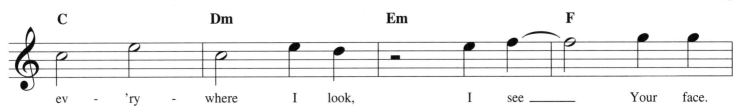

ev - 'ry - where I look, I see _____ Your face.

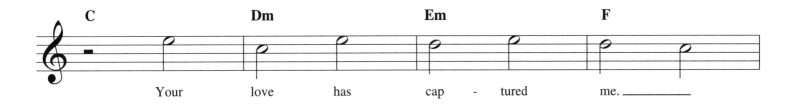

Your love has cap - tured me. _____

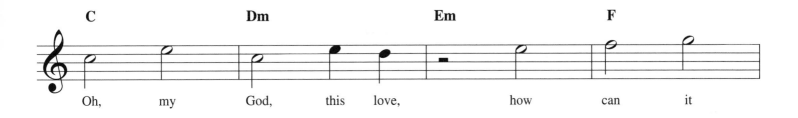

Oh, my God, this love, how can it

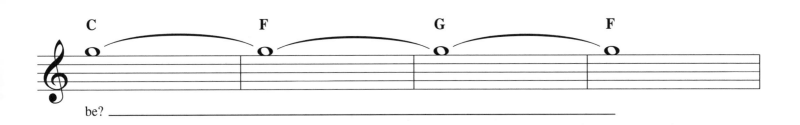

be? _____

La, la, la,

la, la, la, la. La, la, la, la, la, la, la.

FOREVER

Words and Music by
CHRIS TOMLIN

Give   thanks to   the   Lord, ___   our   God   and ___   King. ___   His
With   a   might - y   hand   and   out - stretched __ arm, ___   His
From   the   ris - ing   to   the   set - ting___ sun, ___   His

love   en - dures ____   for - ev - er.
love   en - dures ____   for - ev - er.
love   en - dures ____   for - ev - er.   And   by   the

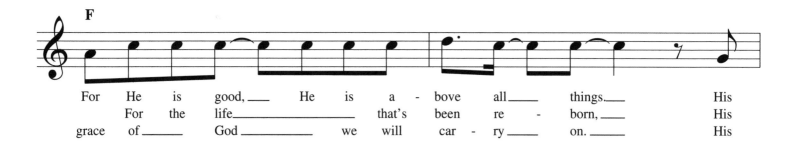

For   He   is   good, ___ He   is   a - bove all ___   things. ___   His
For   the   life_____   that's   been   re - born, ___   His
grace   of ___   God _____   we   will   car - ry ___   on. ___   His

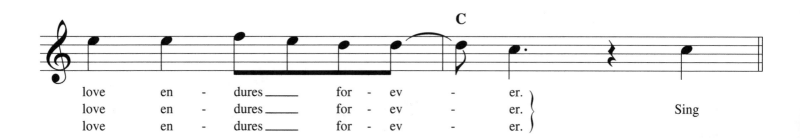

love   en - dures ____   for - ev - er.
love   en - dures ____   for - ev - er.   }
love   en - dures ____   for - ev - er.   }   Sing

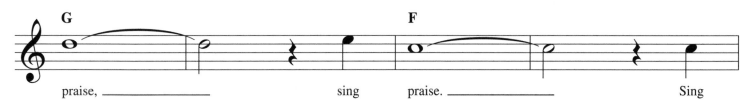

praise, _____ sing praise. _____ Sing

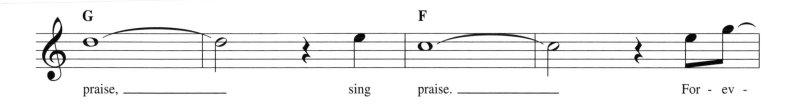

praise, _____ sing praise. _____ For - ev -

- er God _____ is faith - ful, for - ev -

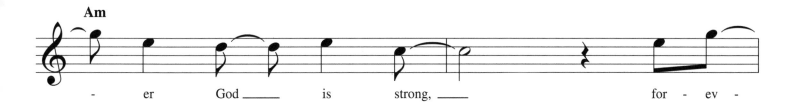

- er God _____ is strong, _____ for - ev -

- er God ___ is with ___ us, for - ev - er, _____

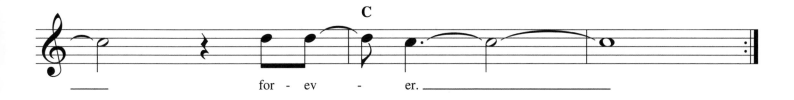

_____ for - ev - er. _____

GIVE THANKS

Words and Music by
HENRY SMITH

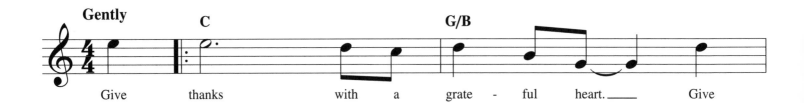

Give thanks with a grate-ful heart.____ Give

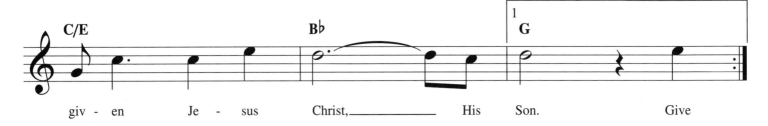

thanks to the Ho-ly One.____ Give thanks____ be-cause He's

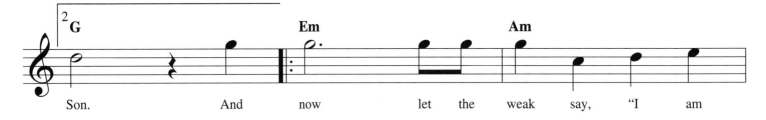

giv-en Je-sus Christ,____ His Son. Give

Son. And now let the weak say, "I am

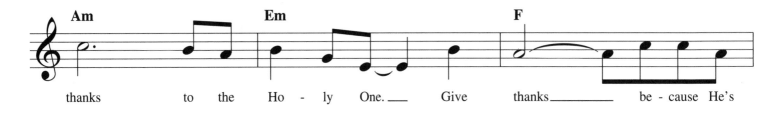

strong," let the poor say, "I am rich," be-cause of

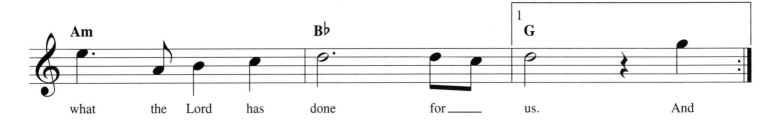

what the Lord has done for____ us. And

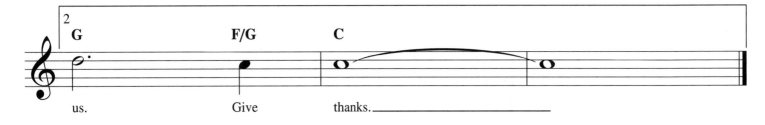

us. Give thanks.____

GLORIFY THY NAME

Words and Music by
DONNA ADKINS

Warmly

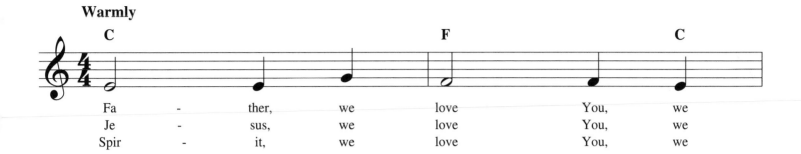

Fa - ther, we love You, we
Je - sus, we love You, we
Spir - it, we love You, we

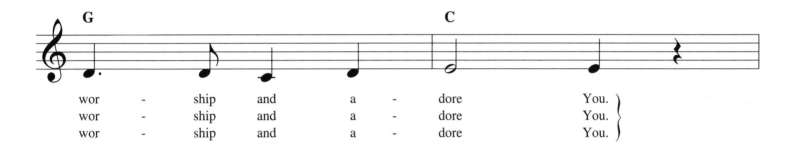

wor - ship and a - dore You.
wor - ship and a - dore You.
wor - ship and a - dore You.

Glo - ri - fy Thy name in all the earth. ____

____ Glo - ri - fy Thy name,

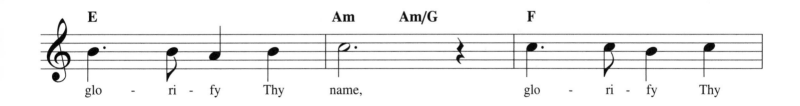

glo - ri - fy Thy name, glo - ri - fy Thy

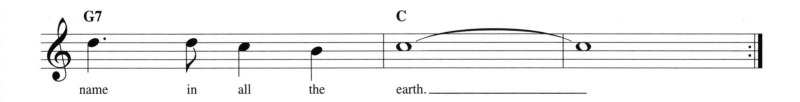

name in all the earth. _____

GOD OF WONDERS

Words and Music by MARC BYRD
and STEVE HINDALONG

With praise

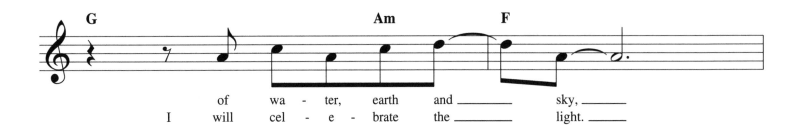

Lord of all cre - a - tion, _____
Ear - ly in the morn - ing _____

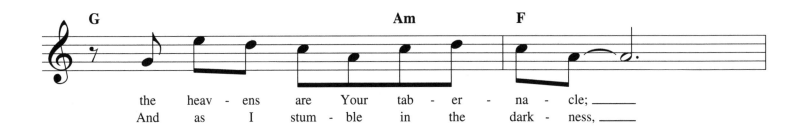

of wa - ter, earth and _____ sky, _____
I will cel - e - brate the _____ light. _____

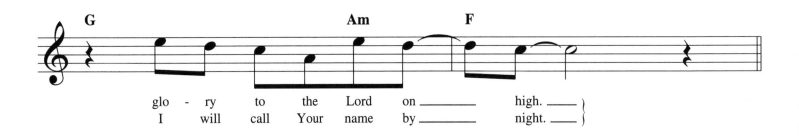

the heav - ens are Your tab - er - na - cle; _____
And as I stum - ble in the dark - ness, _____

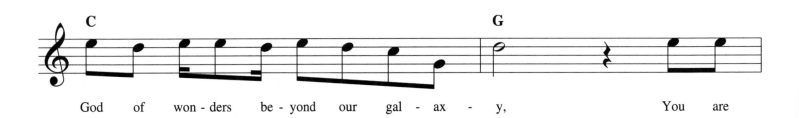

glo - ry to the Lord on _____ high. _____
I will call Your name by _____ night. _____

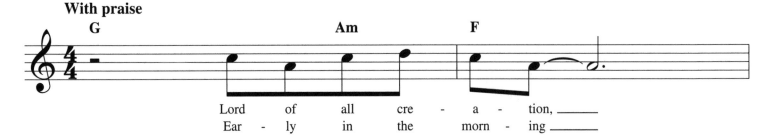

God of won - ders be - yond our gal - ax - y,   You are

ho - ly, ho - ly. The u - ni - verse de - clares Your maj - es -

ty. You are ho - ly, ho - ly;

Lord of heav - en and earth, ___ Lord of heav - en and earth. ___

___ Hal - le - lu - jah ___ to the Lord of ___ heav - en and earth. ___

___ Hal - le - lu - jah ___ to the Lord of ___ heav - en and earth. ___

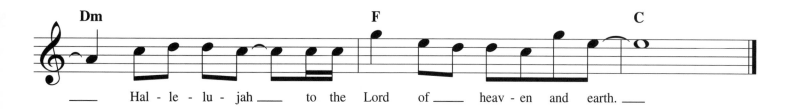

___ Hal - le - lu - jah ___ to the Lord of ___ heav - en and earth. ___

GOD WILL MAKE A WAY

Words and Music by
DON MOEN

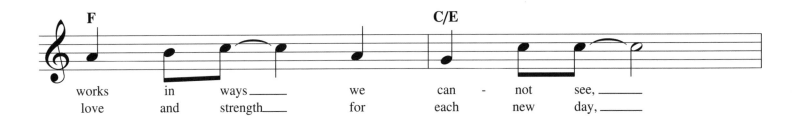

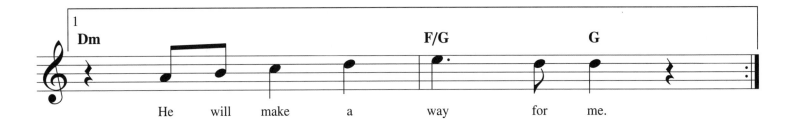

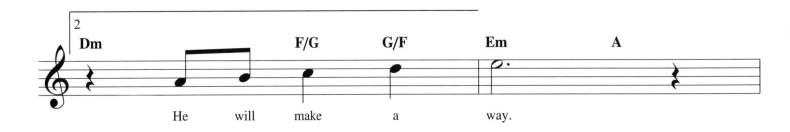

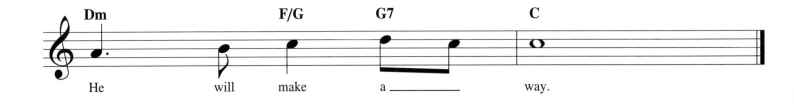

HE HAS MADE ME GLAD

Words and Music by
LEONA VON BRETHORST

Brightly

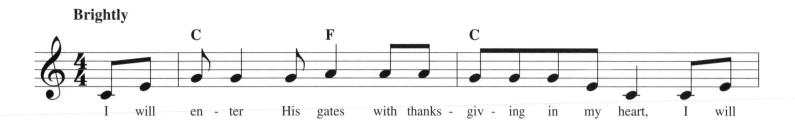

I will en - ter His gates with thanks - giv - ing in my heart, I will

en - ter His courts with praise.___ I will say, "This is the day that the

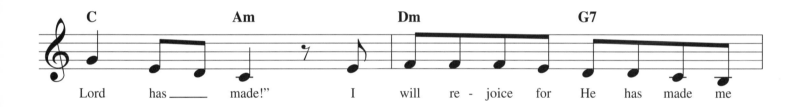

Lord has ___ made!" I will re - joice for He has made me

glad. He has made me glad, He has made me glad, I

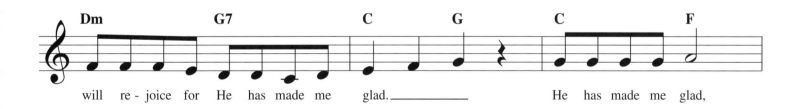

will re - joice for He has made me glad._____ He has made me glad,

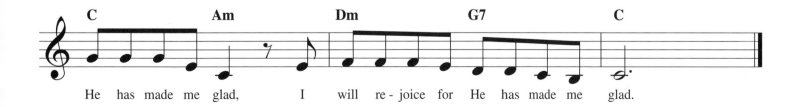

He has made me glad, I will re - joice for He has made me glad.

GREAT IS THE LORD

Words and Music by MICHAEL W. SMITH
and DEBORAH D. SMITH

Flowing

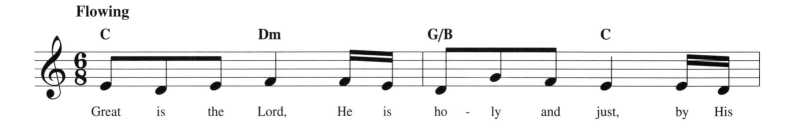

Great is the Lord, He is ho - ly and just, by His

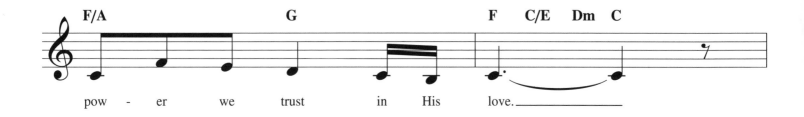

pow - er we trust in His love.

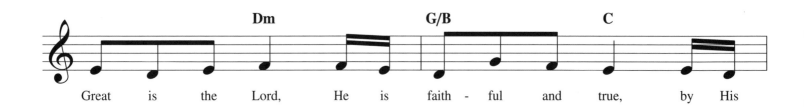

Great is the Lord, He is faith - ful and true, by His

mer - cy He proves He is love.

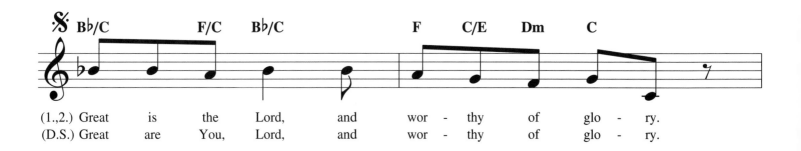

(1.,2.) Great is the Lord, and wor - thy of glo - ry.
(D.S.) Great are You, Lord, and wor - thy of glo - ry.

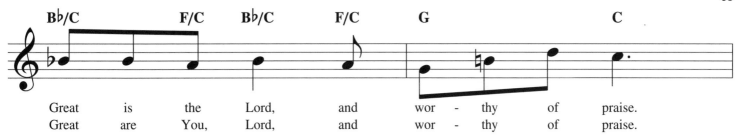

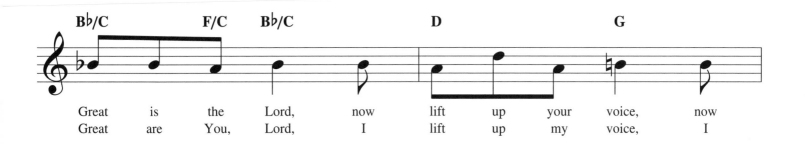

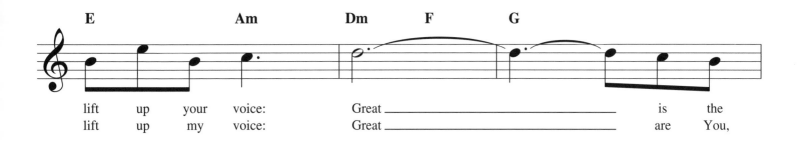

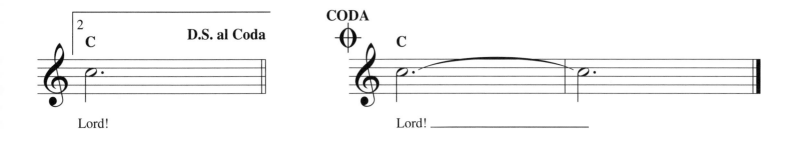

HALLELUJAH
(Your Love Is Amazing)

Words and Music by BRENTON BROWN
and BRIAN DOERKSEN

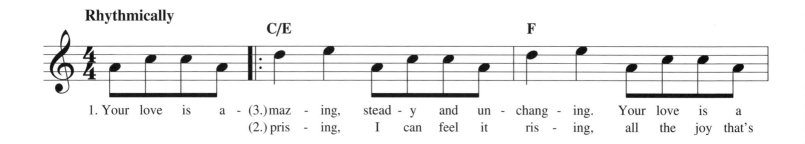

1. Your love is a - (3.)maz - ing, stead - y and un - chang - ing. Your love is a
(2.)pris - ing, I can feel it ris - ing, all the joy that's

moun - tain firm be - neath my feet. Your love is a
grow - ing deep in - side of me. Ev - 'ry time I

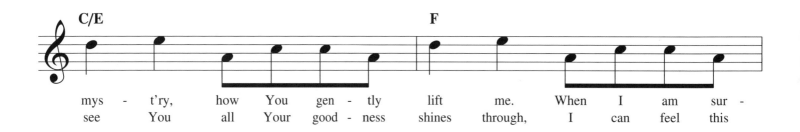

mys - t'ry, how You gen - tly lift me. When I am sur -
see You all Your good - ness shines through, I can feel this

round - ed Your love car - ries me. } Hal - le -
God song ris - ing up in me. }

lu - jah, hal - le - lu - jah, hal - le -

Am   F

lu - jah,   Your love makes me sing. Hal - le -

C   G

lu - jah,   hal - le - lu - jah,   hal - le -

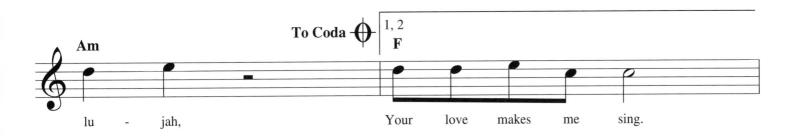

To Coda   1, 2

Am   F

lu - jah,   Your love makes me sing.

3   D.S. al Coda

F

2. Your love is sur -   Your love makes me sing. Hal - le -
3. Your love is a -

CODA

F

Your love makes me sing.   Lord, You make me __

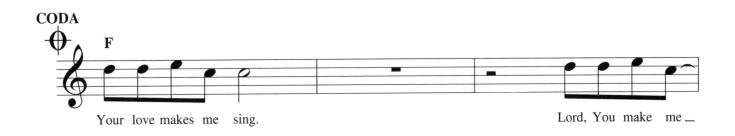

C

__ sing.   How You make me __ sing.

HE IS EXALTED

Words and Music by
TWILA PARIS

Flowing, in 2

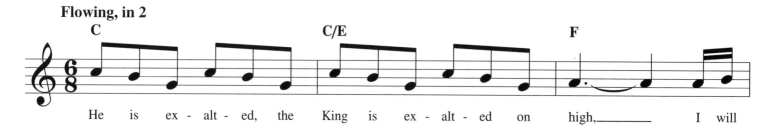

He is ex-alt-ed, the King is ex-alt-ed on high,_____ I will

praise_____ Him. He is ex-alt-ed, for-ev-er ex-alt-ed and

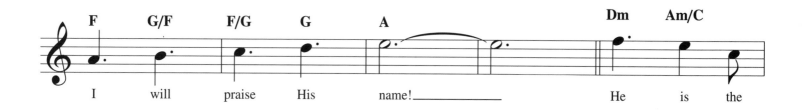

I will praise His name!_____ He is the

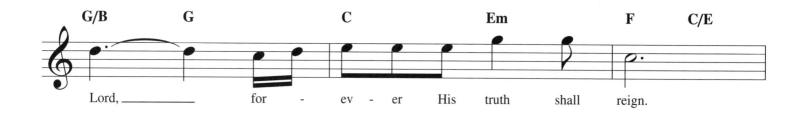

Lord,_____ for-ev-er His truth shall reign.

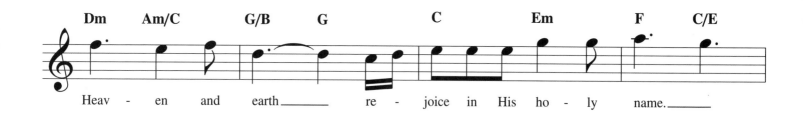

Heav-en and earth_____ re-joice in His ho-ly name._____

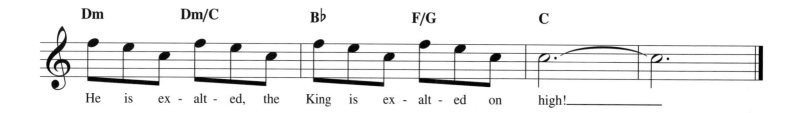

He is ex-alt-ed, the King is ex-alt-ed on high!_____

HE KNOWS MY NAME

Words and Music by
TOMMY WALKER

Moderately slow

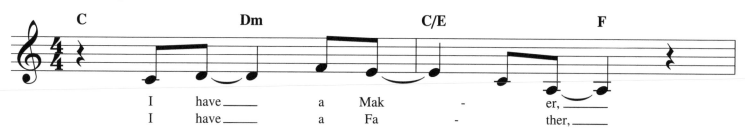

I have _____ a Mak - er, _____
I have _____ a Fa - ther, _____

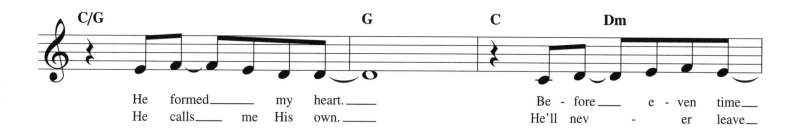

He formed _____ my heart. _____ Be - fore _____ e - ven time _____
He calls _____ me His own. _____ He'll nev - er leave _____

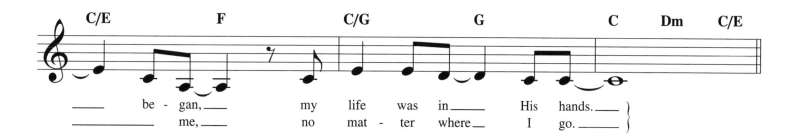

_____ be - gan, _____ my life was in _____ His hands. _____
_____ me, _____ no mat - ter where _____ I go. _____

He knows _____ my name. _____

He knows _ my ev - 'ry thought. _____ He sees _____ each tear _____

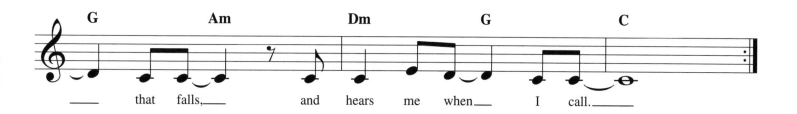

_____ that falls, _____ and hears me when _____ I call.

HEAR OUR PRAISES

Words and Music by
REUBEN MORGAN

Moderately fast

May our homes___ be filled___ with danc - ing,___
May a light___ shine in___ the dark - ness___

may our streets___ be filled___ with joy.___
as we walk___ be - fore___ the cross.___

May in - jus - tice bow___ to Je - sus___
May Your glo - ry fill___ the whole___ earth___

as the peo - ple turn___ to pray.___
as the wa - ter o'er___ the seas.___

From the

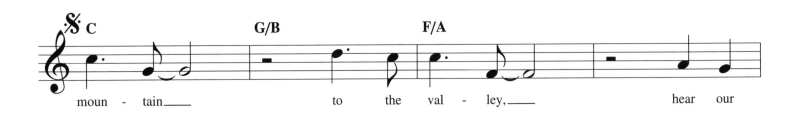

moun - tain___ to the val - ley,___ hear our

prais - es ___ rise to You. From the

heav - ens ___ to the na - tions, ___ hear our

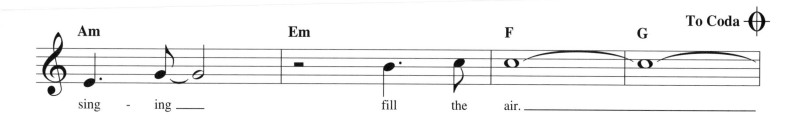

To Coda

sing - ing ___ fill the air. ___

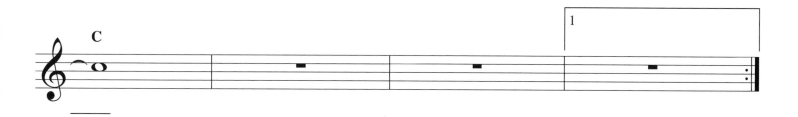

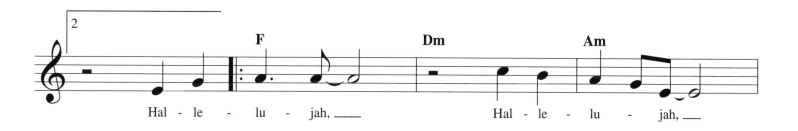

Hal - le - lu - jah, ___ Hal - le - lu - jah, ___

Hal - le - lu - jah, ___ Hal - le - lu - jah! ___

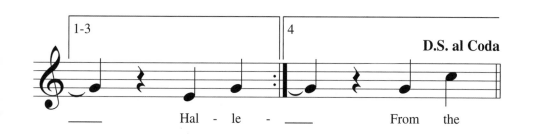

___ Hal - le - ___ From the

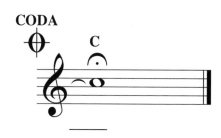

CODA

THE HEART OF WORSHIP

Words and Music by
MATT REDMAN

Steady Ballad

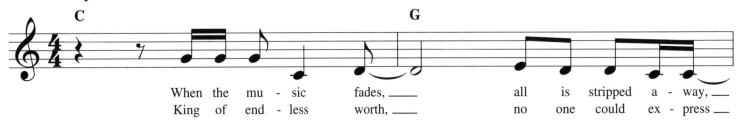

When the mu - sic fades, _____ all is stripped a - way, _____
King of end - less worth, _____ no one could ex - press _____

_____ and I sim - ply come, _____ long - ing just to bring _____
_____ how much You de - serve. _____ Though I'm weak and poor, _____

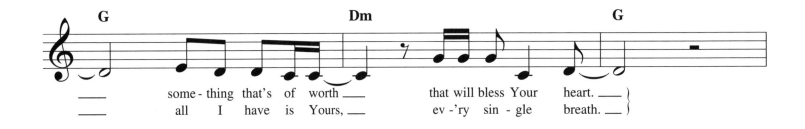

_____ some - thing that's of worth _____ that will bless Your heart. _____
_____ all I have is Yours, _____ ev - 'ry sin - gle breath. _____

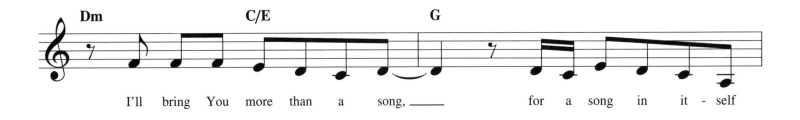

I'll bring You more than a song, _____ for a song in it - self

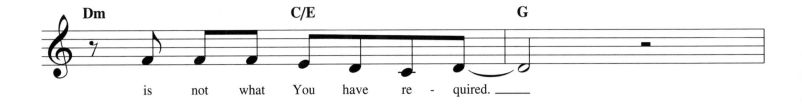

is not what You have re - quired. _____

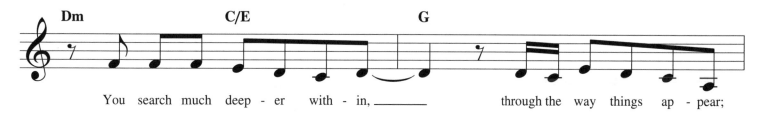

You search much deep - er with - in, _____ through the way things ap - pear;

You're look - ing in - to my heart. _____

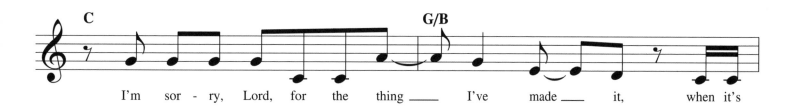

I'm com - ing back to the heart _____ of wor - ship, and it's

all a - bout You, _____ all a - bout You, _____ Je - sus.

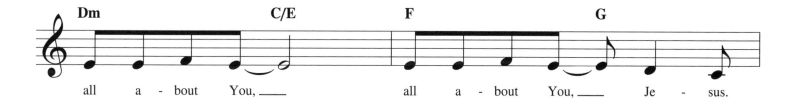

I'm sor - ry, Lord, for the thing _____ I've made _____ it, when it's

all a - bout You, _____ all a - bout You, _____ Je - sus. _____

HERE I AM TO WORSHIP

Words and Music by
TIM HUGHES

Moderately slow, steady

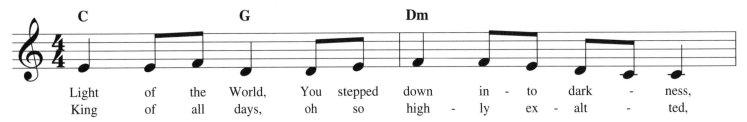

Light of the World, You stepped down in - to dark - ness,
King of all days, oh so high - ly ex - alt - ed,

o - pened my eyes, let me ___ see
glo - rious in heav - en a - bove,

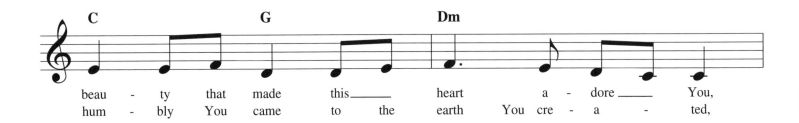

beau - ty that made this ___ heart a - dore ___ You,
hum - bly You came to the earth You cre - a - ted,

hope of a life spent with ___ You.
all for love's sake be - came ___ poor.

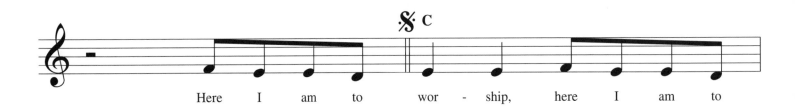

Here I am to wor - ship, here I am to

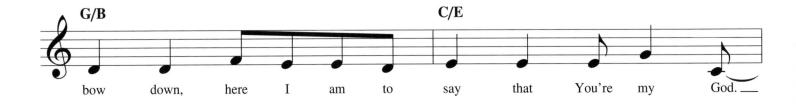

bow down, here I am to say that You're my God. ___

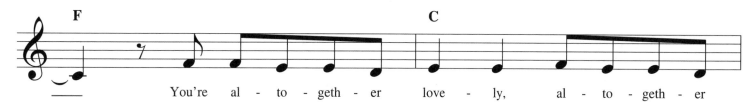

You're al - to - geth - er love - ly, al - to - geth - er

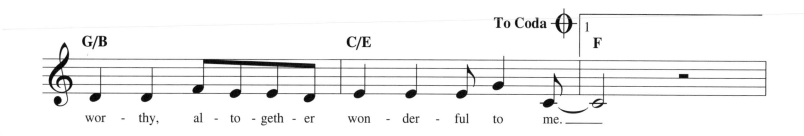

wor - thy, al - to - geth - er won - der - ful to me.

And I'll nev - er know __ how much __

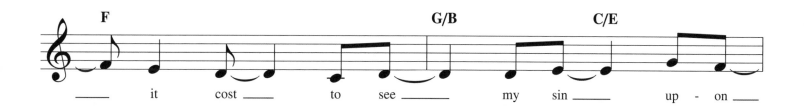

__ it cost __ to see __ my sin __ up - on __

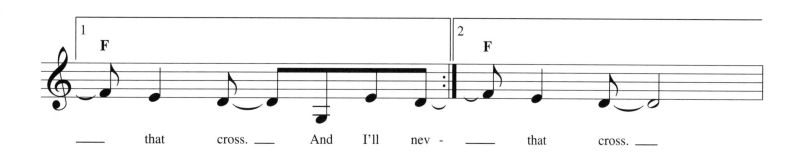

__ that cross. __ And I'll nev - __ that cross. __

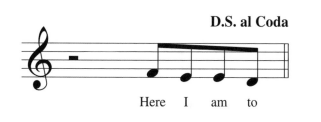

Here I am to

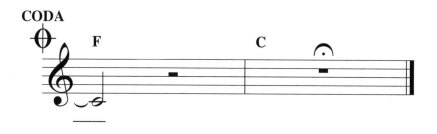

HOLINESS

Words and Music by
SCOTT UNDERWOOD

Prayerfully

Ho - li - ness, ho - li - ness is what I long for. Ho - li - ness is what I
Faith - ful - ness, faith - ful - ness is what I long for. Faith - ful - ness is what I
Bro - ken - ness, bro - ken - ness is what I long for. Bro - ken - ness is what I

need. ___ Ho - li - ness, ho - li - ness is what You want ___ from me. ___
need. ___ Faith - ful - ness, faith - ful - ness is what You want ___ from me. ___
need. ___ Bro - ken - ness, bro - ken - ness is what You want ___ from me. ___

So take my heart ___ and form ___ it. Take my

mind, ___ trans - form ___ it. Take my will, ___ con - form ___ it to Yours, ___

___ to Yours, ___ O ___ Lord. Lord. To Yours, ___ to Yours, ___ O ___

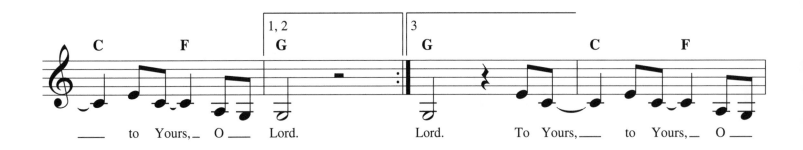

Lord. To Yours, ___ to Yours, ___ O ___ Lord. O ___ Lord.

HOW MAJESTIC IS YOUR NAME

Words and Music by
MICHAEL W. SMITH

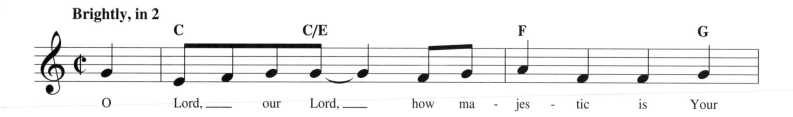

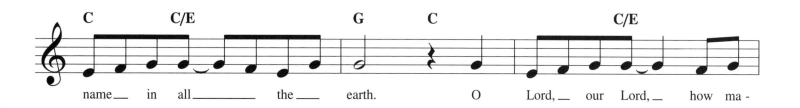

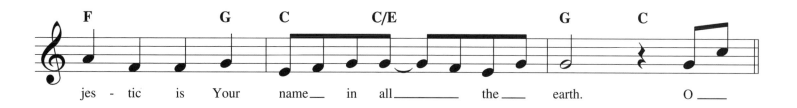

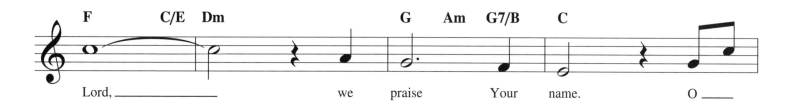

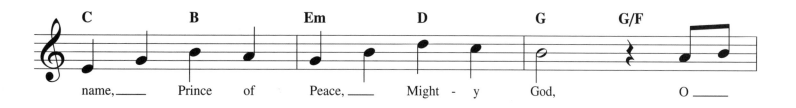

HOLY SPIRIT RAIN DOWN

Words and Music by
RUSSELL FRAGAR

Moderately slow

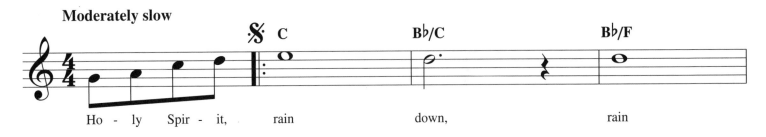

Ho - ly Spir - it, rain down, rain

down. Oh, ___ Com - fort - er ___ and Friend, ___ how we

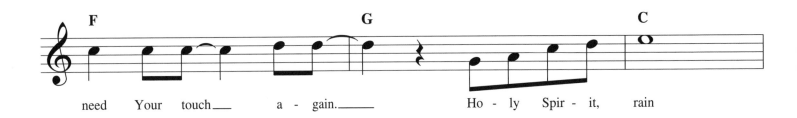

need Your touch ___ a - gain. ___ Ho - ly Spir - it, rain

down, rain down. Let Your pow - er fall, ___ let Your

voice be heard. ___ Come and change our hearts, ___ as we

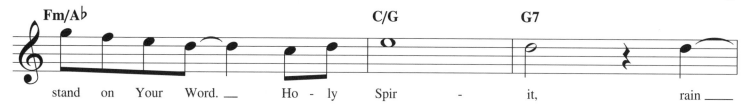

stand on Your Word. ___ Ho - ly Spir - it, rain ____

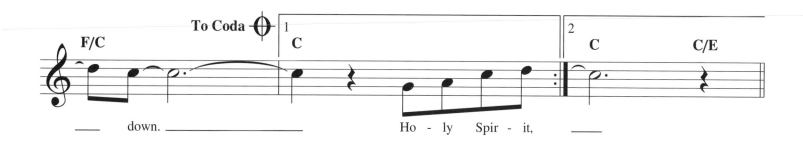

___ down. _____ Ho - ly Spir - it, ____

No eye has seen, ___ no ear has heard, _ no mind can know ___ what

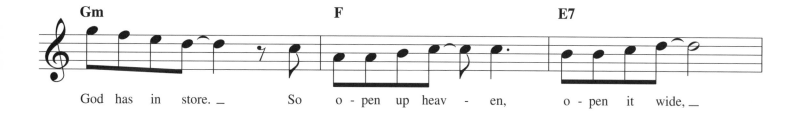

God has in store. _ So o - pen up heav - en, o - pen it wide, ___

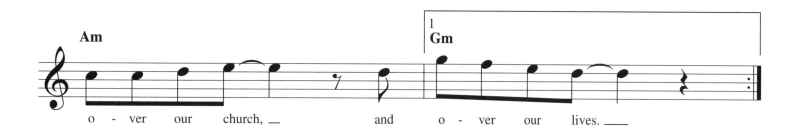

o - ver our church, ___ and o - ver our lives. ___

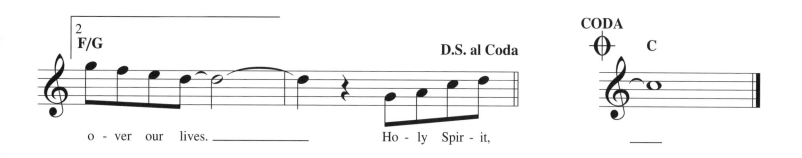

o - ver our lives. _____ Ho - ly Spir - it,

HUNGRY
(Falling on My Knees)

Words and Music by
KATHRYN SCOTT

I EXALT THEE

Words and Music by
PETE SANCHEZ, JR.

Moderately

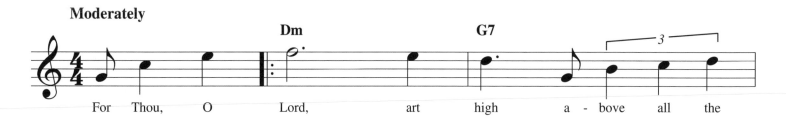

For Thou, O Lord, art high a - bove all the

earth. _____ Thou art ex - alt - ed far a -

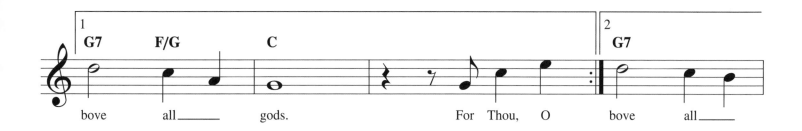

bove all _____ gods. For Thou, O bove all _____

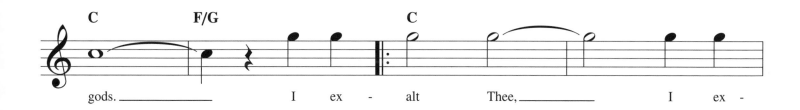

gods. _____ I ex - alt Thee, _____ I ex -

alt _____ Thee, _____ I ex - alt _____ Thee, _____ O _____

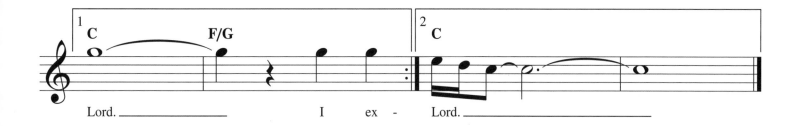

Lord. _____ I ex - Lord. _____

I COULD SING OF YOUR LOVE FOREVER

Words and Music by
MARTIN SMITH

Moderately

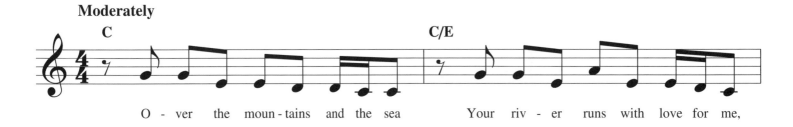

O - ver the moun - tains and the sea   Your riv - er runs with love for me,

and I will o - pen up my heart and let the Heal - er set me free.

I'm hap - py to be in the truth   and I will dai - ly lift my hands,

for I will al - ways sing of when Your love came down. _____

I could sing of Your love _____ for - ev - er.

I could sing of Your love _____ for - ev - er.

71

I could sing of Your love _____ for - ev - er.

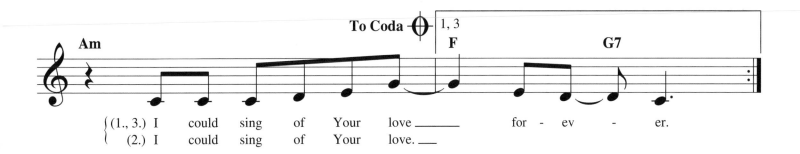

{ (1., 3.) I could sing of Your love _____ for - ev - er.
  (2.) I could sing of Your love. __

___ Oh, I feel like danc - ing.

It's fool - ish - ness, I know. _____ But when the world has

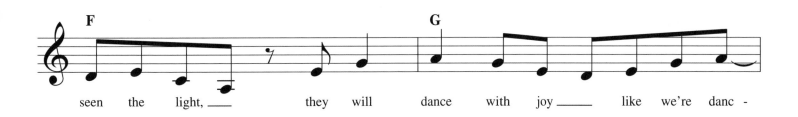

seen the light, ___ they will dance with joy ___ like we're danc -

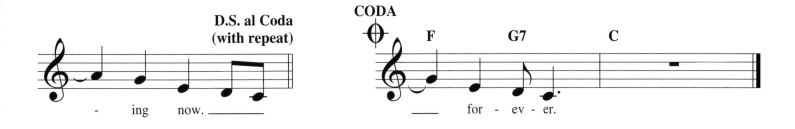

- ing now. _____ ___ for - ev - er.

I GIVE YOU MY HEART

Words and Music by
REUBEN MORGAN

Moderately

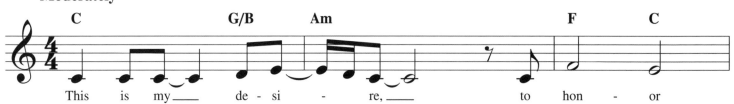

This is my ___ de - si - re, ___ to hon - or

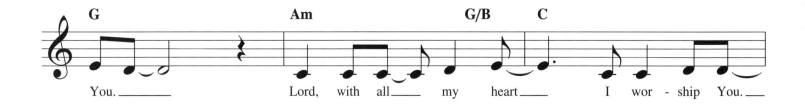

You. ___ Lord, with all ___ my heart ___ I wor - ship You. ___

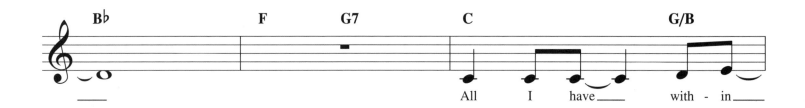

___ All I have ___ with - in ___

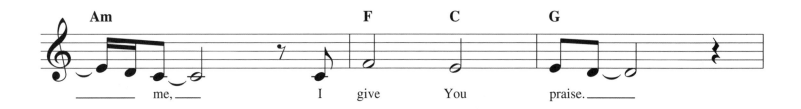

___ me, ___ I give You praise. ___

All that I ___ a - dore ___ is in You. ___

Lord, I give You my heart, ___

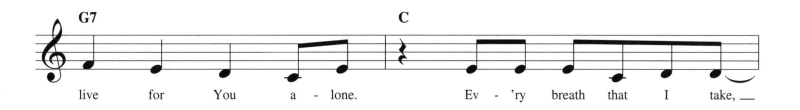

___ I give You my ___ soul. ___ I

live for You a - lone. Ev - 'ry breath that I take, ___

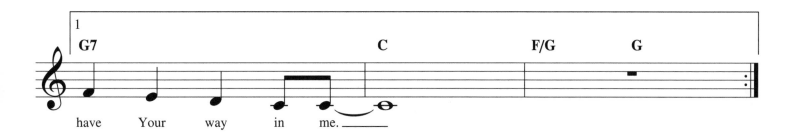

___ ev - 'ry mo - ment I'm ___ a - wake, ___ Lord,

have Your way in me. ___

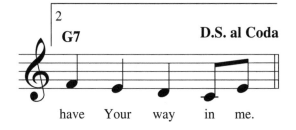

have Your way in me.

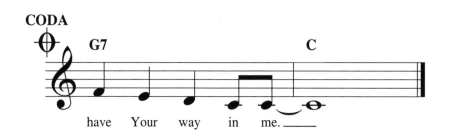

have Your way in me. ___

I LOVE YOU LORD

Words and Music by
MARTIN NYSTROM

Warmly

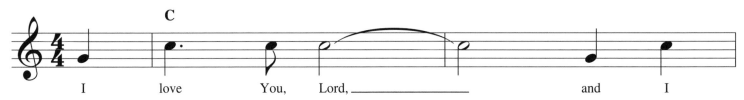

I love You, Lord, _____ and I

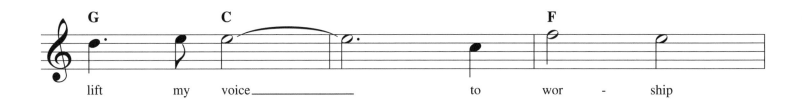

lift my voice_____ to wor - ship

You.   O my soul, re - joice!   Take

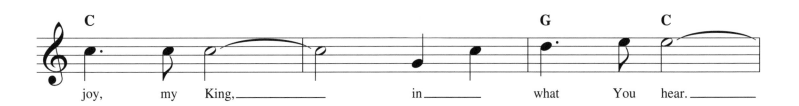

joy, my King,_____ in_____ what You hear._____

_____ May it be a sweet, sweet_____

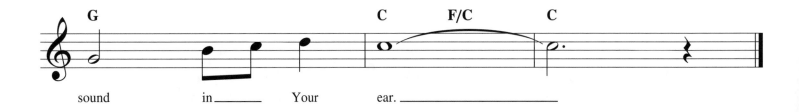

sound in_____ Your ear._____

I SING PRAISES

Words and Music by
TERRY MacALMON

Moderately

I sing prais - es to Your name, O ____ Lord, prais - es to Your
I give glo - ry to Your name, O ____ Lord, glo - ry to Your

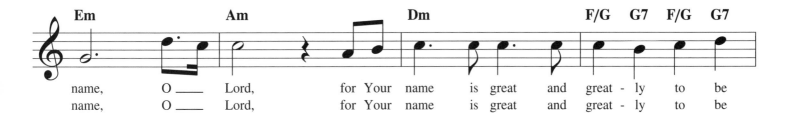

name, O ____ Lord, for Your name is great and great - ly to be
name, O ____ Lord, for Your name is great and great - ly to be

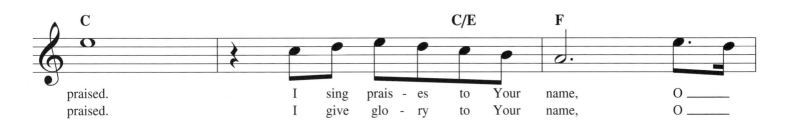

praised. I sing prais - es to Your name, O ____
praised. I give glo - ry to Your name, O ____

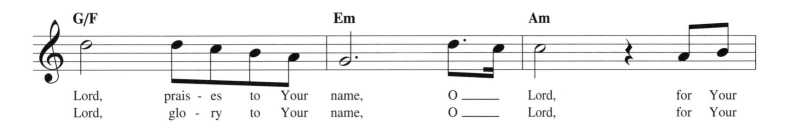

Lord, prais - es to Your name, O ____ Lord, for Your
Lord, glo - ry to Your name, O ____ Lord, for Your

name is great and great - ly to be praised.
name is great and great - ly to be praised.

I STAND IN AWE

Words and Music by
MARK ALTROGGE

I WILL CALL UPON THE LORD

Words and Music by
MICHAEL O'SHIELDS

Moderately

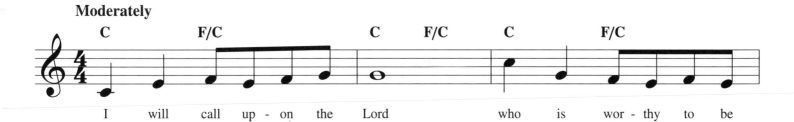

I will call up-on the Lord who is wor-thy to be

praised. So shall I be saved from my en-e-mies.___

___ I will call up-on the Lord. The

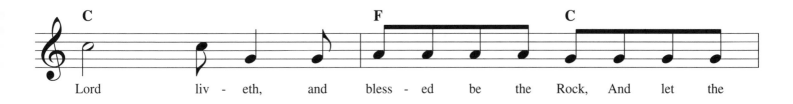

Lord liv-eth, and bless-ed be the Rock, And let the

God of my sal-va-tion be ex-alt-ed. The

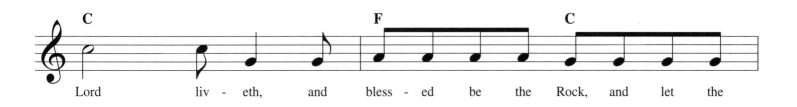

Lord liv-eth, and bless-ed be the Rock, and let the

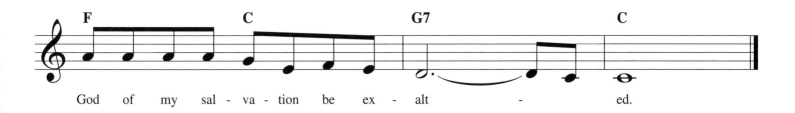

God of my sal-va-tion be ex-alt-ed.

I WANT TO KNOW YOU

Words and Music by
ANDY PARK

Moderately slow, in 2

In the se - cret, in the qui - et place, ___
I am reach - ing for the high - est goal, ___

___ in the still - ness
___ that I might ___ re -

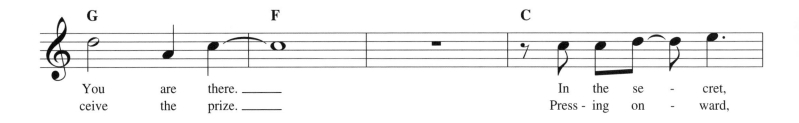

You are there. _____ In the se - cret,
ceive the prize. _____ Press - ing on - ward,

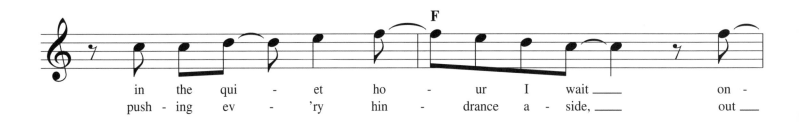

in the qui - et ho - ur I wait ___ on -
push - ing ev - 'ry hin - drance a - side, ___ out ___

- ly for You, ___ 'cause I want ___ to know You
___ of my way, ___ 'cause I want ___ to know You

more. _____
more. _____

I want to

know You, _____ I want to hear Your _____ voice.

I want to know You _____ more. _____

_____ I want to touch You, _____

I want to see Your _____ face. I want to

know You _____ more. _____

I WORSHIP YOU, ALMIGHTY GOD

Words and Music by
SONDRA CORBETT-WOOD

Moderately, not too slow

I wor - ship You, Al - might - y God; there is none like

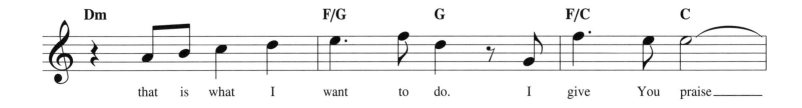

You. I wor - ship You, O Prince of Peace;

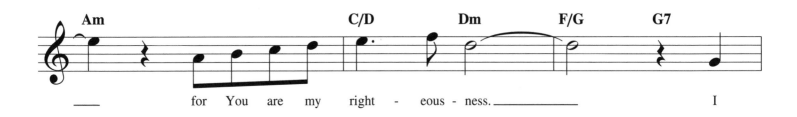

that is what I want to do. I give You praise_____

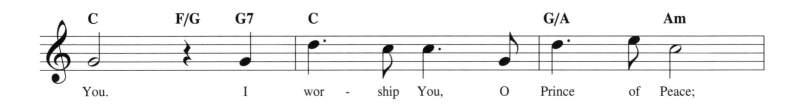

_____ for You are my right - eous - ness._____ I

wor - ship You, Al - might - y God; there is none like You.

IN HIS PRESENCE

Words and Music by DICK TUNNEY
and MELODIE TUNNEY

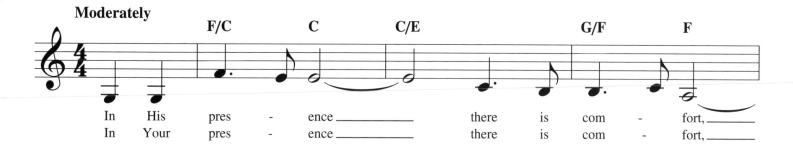

In His pres - ence _____ there is com - fort, _____
In Your pres - ence _____ there is com - fort, _____

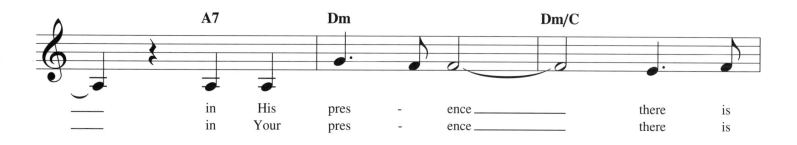

_____ in His pres - ence _____ there is
_____ in Your pres - ence _____ there is

peace. _____ When we seek the Fa - ther's _____
peace. _____ When we seek to know Your _____

heart, we will find such blessed as - sur - ance in the
heart, we will find such blessed as - sur - ance in Your

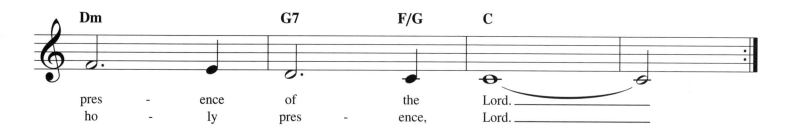

pres - ence of the Lord. _____
ho - ly pres - ence, Lord. _____

IN CHRIST ALONE

Words and Music by KEITH GETTY
and STUART TOWNEND

Moderately slow

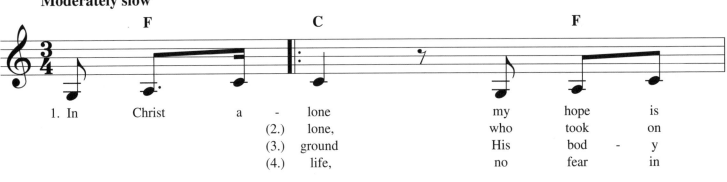

1. In   Christ   a - lone   my   hope   is
(2.) lone,   who   took   on
(3.) ground   His   bod - y
(4.) life,   no   fear   in

found,   He   is   my   light,   my   strength,   my
flesh,   full - ness of   God   in   help - less
lay,   Light of   the   world   by   dark - ness
death;   this   is   the   pow'r   of   Christ   in

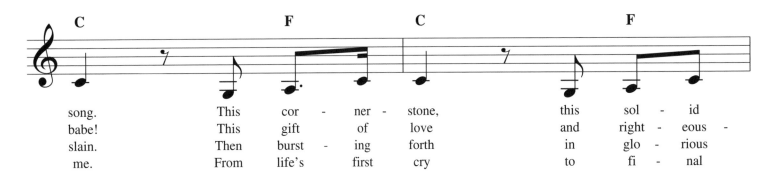

song.   This   cor - ner - stone,   this   sol - id
babe!   This   gift   of   love   and   right - eous -
slain.   Then   burst - ing forth   in   glo - rious
me.   From   life's first cry   to   fi - nal

ground,   firm   through the   fierc - est   drought   and
ness,   scorned by   the   ones   He   came   to
day,   up   from   the   grave   He   rose   a -
breath,   Je -   sus   com - mands   my   des -   ti -

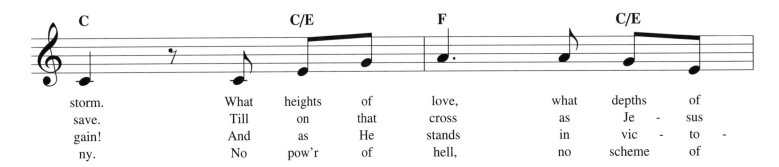

storm.   What   heights of   love,   what   depths   of
save.   Till   on   that cross   as   Je   -   sus
gain!   And   as   He   stands   in   vic -   to -
ny.   No   pow'r   of   hell,   no   scheme   of

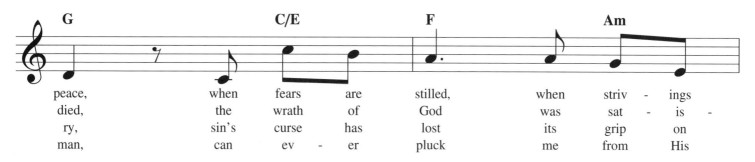

peace,   when fears are stilled,   when striv - ings
died,   the wrath of God   was sat - is -
ry,   sin's curse has lost   its grip on
man,   can ev - er pluck   me from His

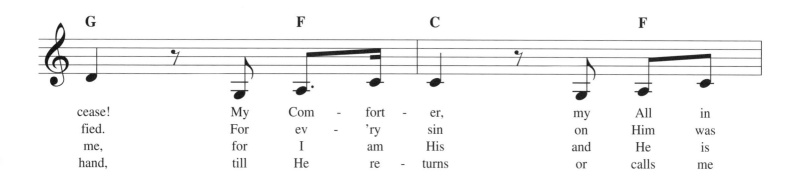

cease!   My Com - fort - er,   my All in
fied.   For ev - 'ry sin   on Him was
me,   for I am His   and He is
hand,   till He re - turns   or calls me

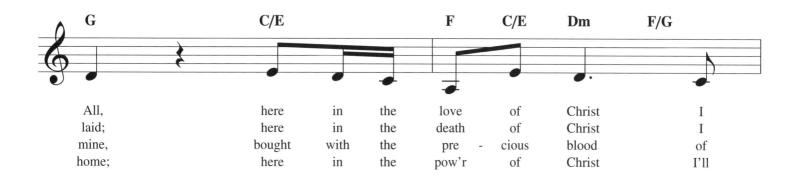

All,   here in the love of Christ I
laid;   here in the death of Christ I
mine,   bought with the pre - cious blood of
home;   here in the pow'r of Christ I'll

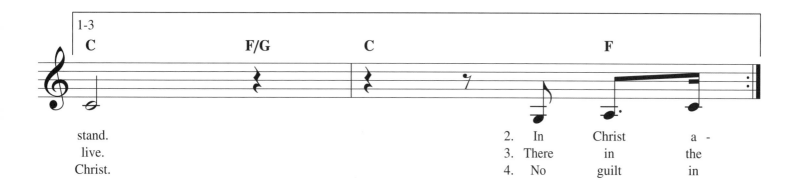

stand.   2. In Christ a -
live.   3. There in the
Christ.   4. No guilt in

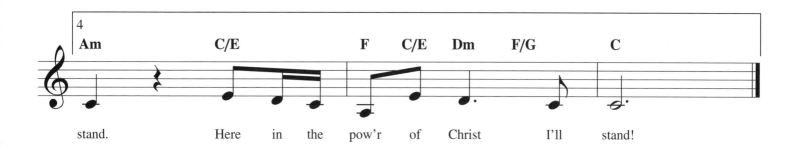

stand.   Here in the pow'r of Christ I'll stand!

IT IS YOU

Words and Music by
PETER FURLER

Moderately slow

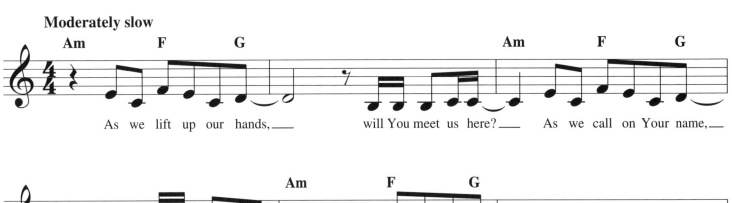

As we lift up our hands, ___ will You meet us here? ___ As we call on Your name, ___

___ will You meet us here? ___ We have come to this place ___ to wor-ship You, ___

___ God of mer-cy and grace. ___ It is You ___ we a-dore. ___ It is You ___

___ prais-es are for, ___ on-ly You. ___ The heav-ens de-clare ___

___ it is You, ___ it is You. ___ And ho-ly, ho-ly is our

God Al-might - y, ___ and ho-ly, ho-ly is His name a-lone, yeah, ___

To Coda ⊕

And ho-ly, ho-ly is our God Al-might - y, ___ and ho-ly, ho-ly is His

name a - lone. It is You ____ we a - dore. ____ It is You, ____ on - ly You. ___

___ name a - lone. As we lift _____ up our hands, as we call ___

___ on Your name, will You vis - it this place by Your mer - cy and grace? As we lift ___

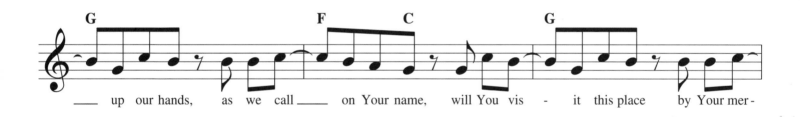

___ up our hands, as we call ____ on Your name, will You vis - it this place by Your mer-

- cy and grace? It is You ____ we a - dore. ___ It is You. ___

D.S. al Coda

CODA

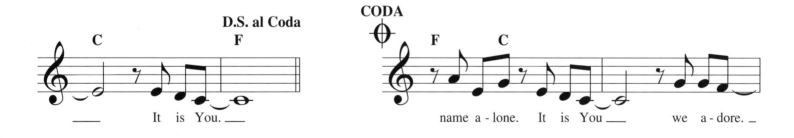

It is You. ___   name a - lone. It is You ____ we a - dore. ___

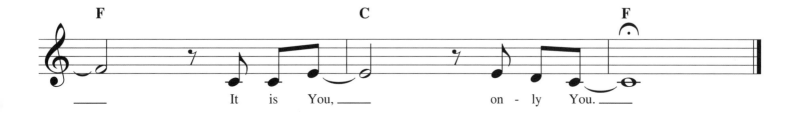

___ It is You, ____ on - ly You. ____

JESUS, LOVER OF MY SOUL

Words and Music by JOHN EZZY, DANIEL GRUL
and STEPHEN McPHERSON

Moderate Ballad

Je - sus, lov - er of my soul,_____ Je - sus, I will

nev - er let You go._____ You've tak - en me____ from the mir - y clay,_____

set my feet up - on____ the rock, and now I know_____

I love You, I need___ You. Though my world may fall,___ I'll

nev - er let____ You go._____ My Sav - ior, my clos - est Friend,__

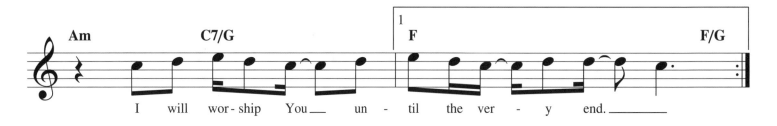

I will wor - ship You___ un - til the ver - y end._____

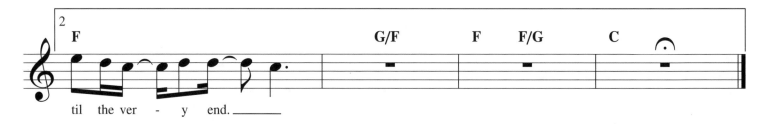

til the ver - y end._____

JESUS, NAME ABOVE ALL NAMES

Words and Music by
NAIDA HEARN

Smoothly

Je - sus, _____ name a - bove all names, _____

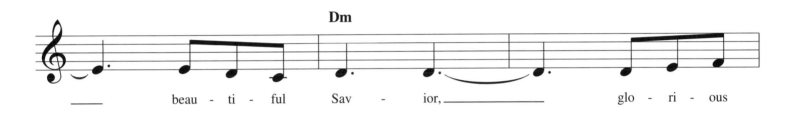

_____ beau - ti - ful Sav - ior, _____ glo - ri - ous

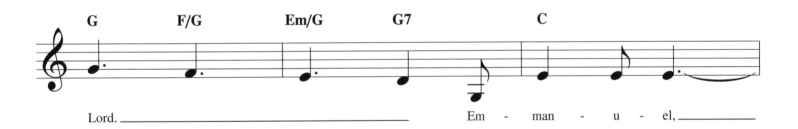

Lord. _____ Em - man - u - el, _____

_____ God ____ is with us, _____ bless - ed Re -

deem - er, _____ liv - ing Word. _____

KNOWING YOU
(All I Once Held Dear)

Words and Music by
GRAHAM KENDRICK

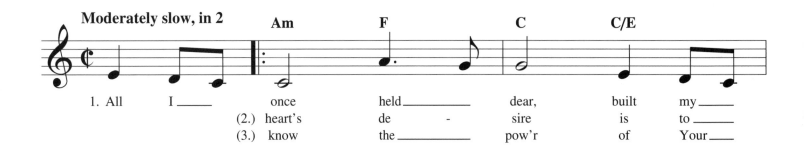

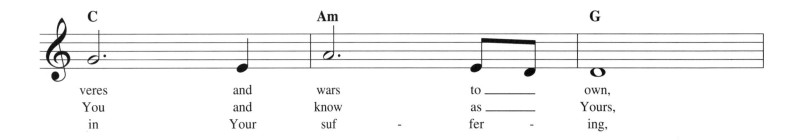

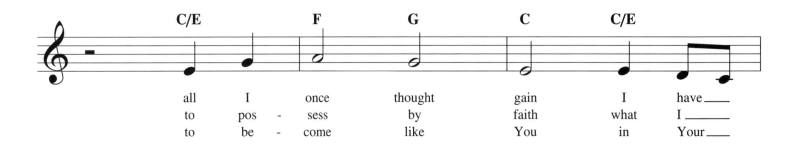

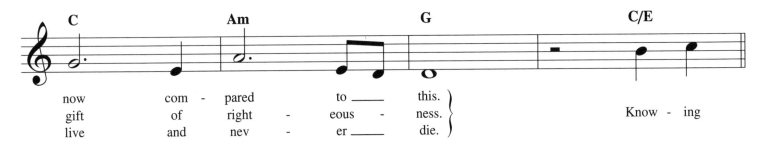

now com - pared to ___ this.
gift of right - eous - ness.
live and nev - er ___ die. Know - ing

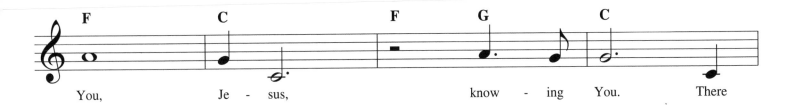

You, Je - sus, know - ing You. There

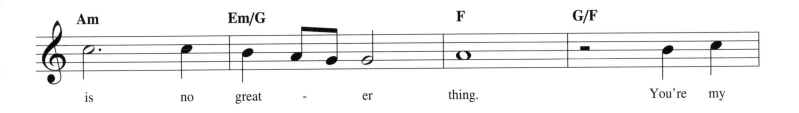

is no great - er thing. You're my

all, You're the best, ___ You're my joy, my right - eous - ness; _

___ and I love You, Lord. ___

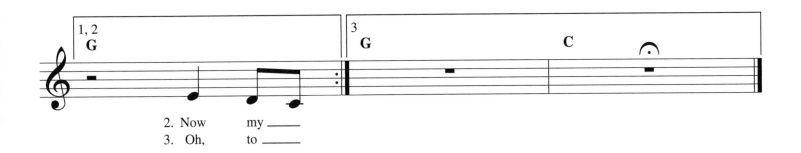

2. Now my ___
3. Oh, to ___

LAMB OF GOD

Words and Music by
TWILA PARIS

With emotion

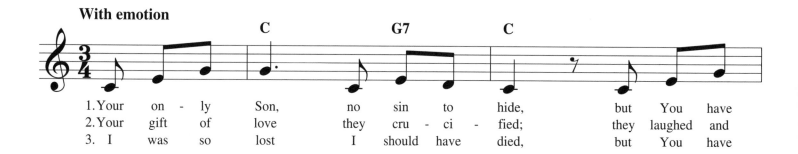

1. Your on - ly Son, no sin to hide, but You have
2. Your gift of love they cru - ci - fied; they laughed and
3. I was so lost I should have died, but You have

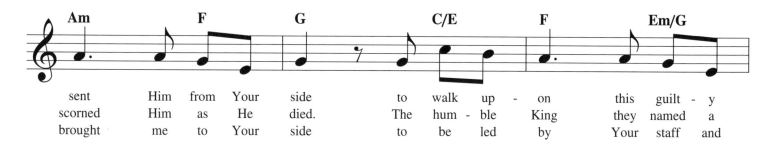

sent Him from Your side to walk up - on this guilt - y
scorned Him as He died. The hum - ble King they named a
brought me to Your side to be led by Your staff and

sod, and to be - come the Lamb of God.
fraud, and sac - ri - ficed the Lamb of God.   O ___ Lamb __ of ___
rod, and to be called a lamb of God.

God ___ sweet _ Lamb of God; I love the ho - ly Lamb of

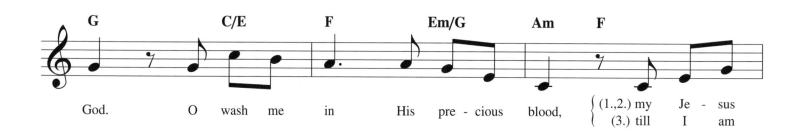

God. O wash me in His pre - cious blood, (1.,2.) my Je - sus
(3.) till I am

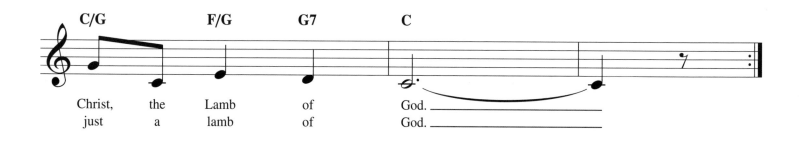

Christ, the Lamb of God. ___
just a lamb of God. ___

LORD, BE GLORIFIED

Words and Music by
BOB KILPATRICK

Moderately slow

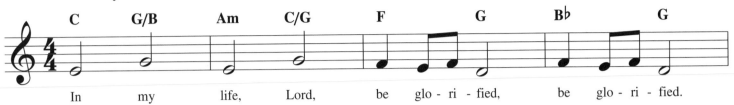

In my life, Lord, be glo-ri-fied, be glo-ri-fied.

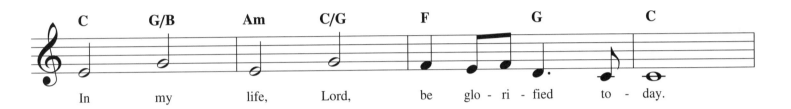

In my life, Lord, be glo-ri-fied to-day.

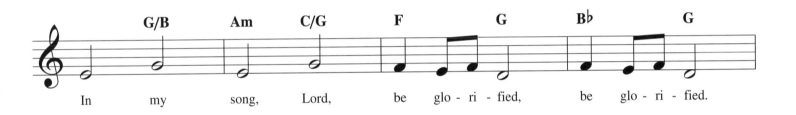

In my song, Lord, be glo-ri-fied, be glo-ri-fied.

In my song, Lord, be glo-ri-fied to-day.

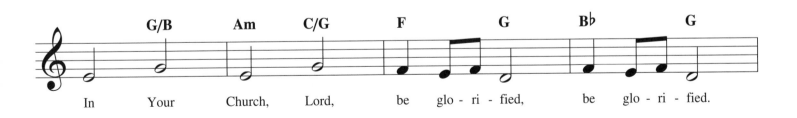

In Your Church, Lord, be glo-ri-fied, be glo-ri-fied.

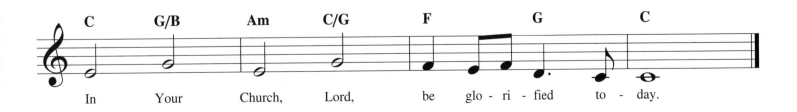

In Your Church, Lord, be glo-ri-fied to-day.

LORD, I LIFT YOUR NAME ON HIGH

Words and Music by
RICK FOUNDS

Brightly

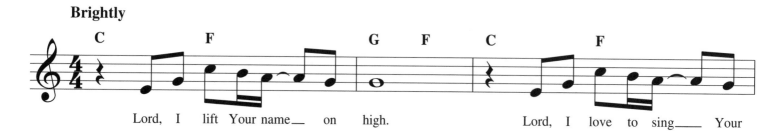

Lord, I lift Your name___ on high. Lord, I love to sing___ Your

prais - es. I'm so glad You're in___ my life.

I'm so glad You came___ to save___ us. You came from heav - en to earth___

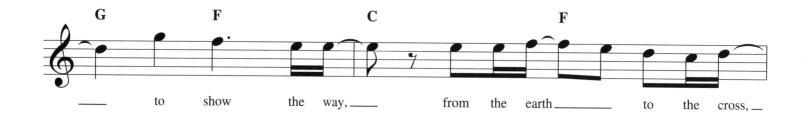

___ to show the way, ___ from the earth___ to the cross, ___

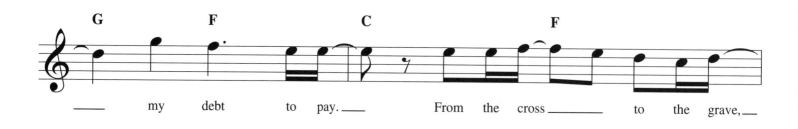

___ my debt to pay. ___ From the cross___ to the grave, ___

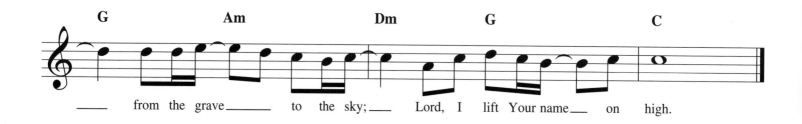

___ from the grave___ to the sky; ___ Lord, I lift Your name___ on high.

MIGHTY IS OUR GOD

Words and Music by EUGENE GRECO,
GERRIT GUSTAFSON and DON MOEN

Driving

Might - y is ___ our God, ___ might - y is ___ our King, ___
Glo - ry to ___ our God, ___ glo - ry to ___ our King, _

To Coda

___ might - y is ___ our Lord, ___
___ glo - ry to ___ our Lord, ___

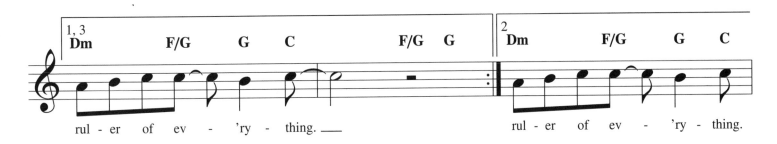

rul - er of ev - 'ry - thing. ___ rul - er of ev - 'ry - thing.

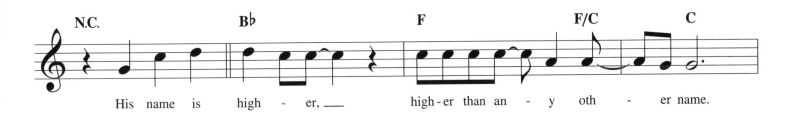

His name is high - er, ___ high - er than an - y oth - er name.

His pow'r is great - er, ___ for He has cre - at - ed ev -

**D.C. al Coda
(with repeat)**

- 'ry - thing.

CODA

rul - er of ev - 'ry - thing. ___

LORD, REIGN IN ME

Words and Music by
BRENTON BROWN

Steady acoustic feel

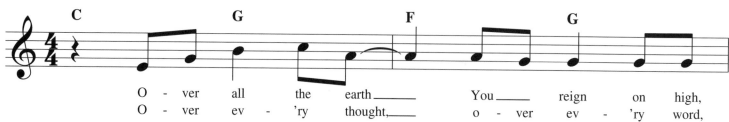

O - ver all the earth_____ You_____ reign on high,
O - ver ev - 'ry thought,_____ o - ver ev - 'ry word,

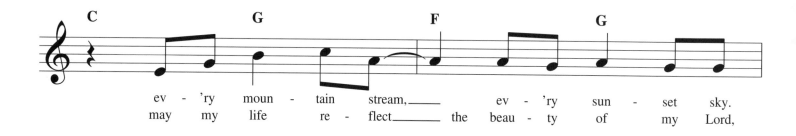

ev - 'ry moun - tain stream,_____ ev - 'ry sun - set sky.
may my life re - flect_____ the beau - ty of my Lord,

But my one re - quest,_____ Lord, my on - ly aim_____
'cause You mean more to me_____ than an - y earth - ly thing,_____

_____ is that You'd reign in me a - gain.
_____ so won't You reign in me a - gain?

Lord, reign in me,_____ reign in Your pow'r,

o - ver all my dreams, ____ in my dark - est hour.

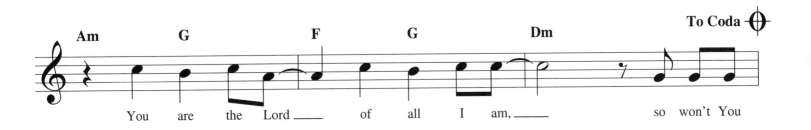

You are the Lord ____ of all I am, ____ so won't You

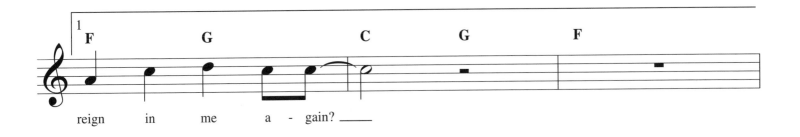

reign in me a - gain? ____

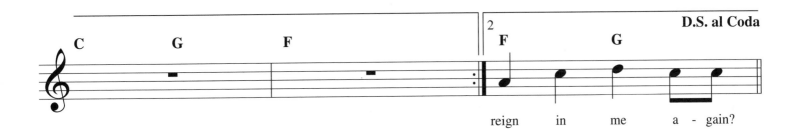

reign in me a - gain?

reign in me a - gain? _____

MAJESTY

Words and Music by
JACK W. HAYFORD

Broadly

Maj - es - ty, _____ wor - ship His

maj - es - ty. _____ Un - to Je - sus be all

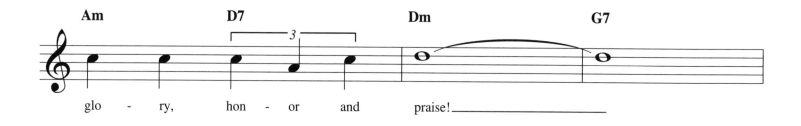

glo - ry, hon - or and praise! _____

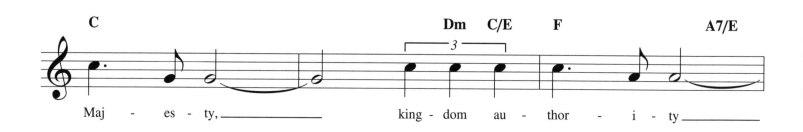

Maj - es - ty, _____ king - dom au - thor - i - ty _____

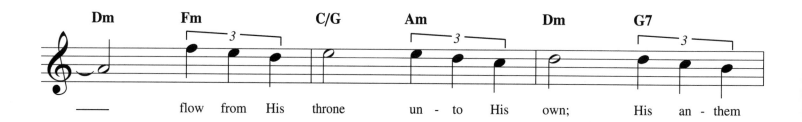

_____ flow from His throne un - to His own; His an - them

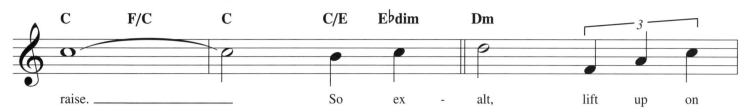

raise. _____ So ex - alt, lift up on

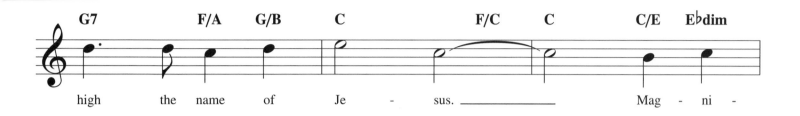

high the name of Je - sus. _____ Mag - ni -

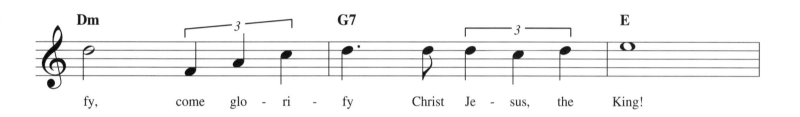

fy, come glo - ri - fy Christ Je - sus, the King!

(Instrumental) Maj - es - ty, _____ wor - ship His

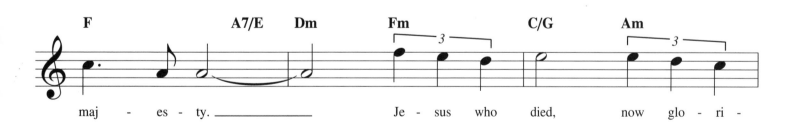

maj - es - ty. _____ Je - sus who died, now glo - ri -

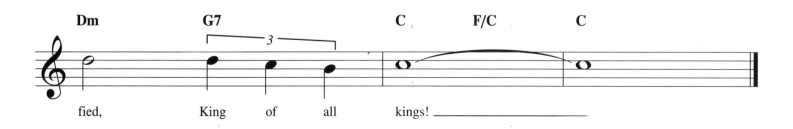

fied, King of all kings! _____

MORE LOVE, MORE POWER

Words and Music by
EDDIE ESPINOSA

Moderately

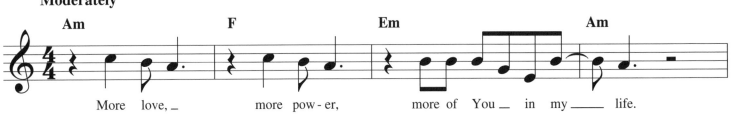

More love, — more pow-er, more of You — in my ___ life.

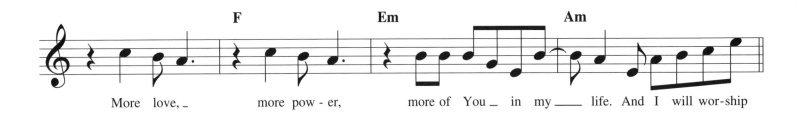

More love, — more pow-er, more of You — in my ___ life. And I will wor-ship

(1., 2.) You with all of my heart, ___ and I will wor-ship You with all of my mind, —
(3.) praise with all of my heart, ___ and I will sing Your praise with all of my mind, —

___ and I will wor-ship You with all of my strength, — for You are my Lord. —
___ and I will sing Your praise with all of my strength, — for You are my Lord. —

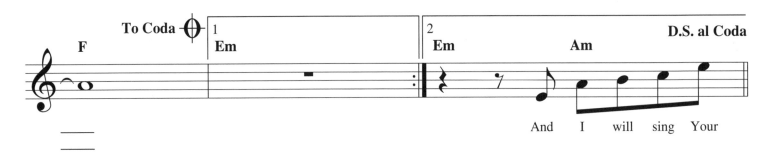

And I will sing Your

CODA

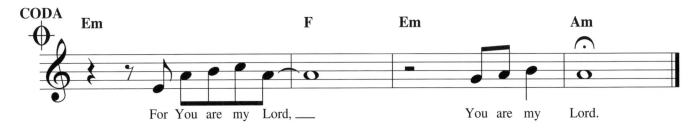

For You are my Lord, ___ You are my Lord.

MORE PRECIOUS THAN SILVER

Words and Music by
LYNN DeSHAZO

Warmly

Lord, You are more pre - cious than

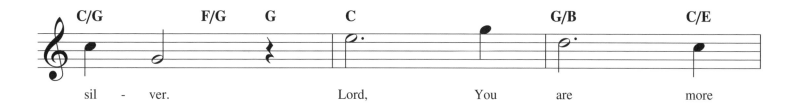

sil - ver. Lord, You are more

cost - ly than gold. Lord, You

are more beau - ti - ful_____ than dia - monds, and

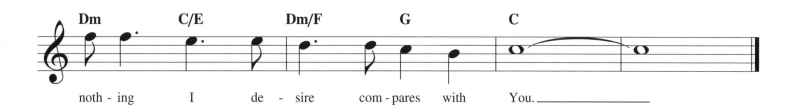

noth - ing I de - sire com - pares with You._____

MY LIFE IS IN YOU, LORD

Words and Music by
DANIEL GARDNER

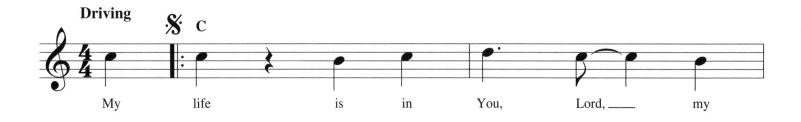

My life is in You, Lord, ___ my

strength is in You, Lord, _ my hope is in

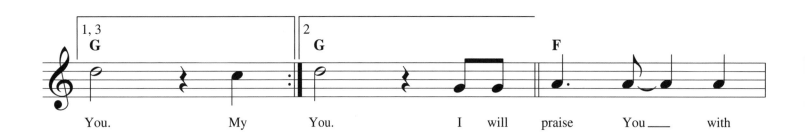

You, Lord, ___ in You, _____ it's in ___

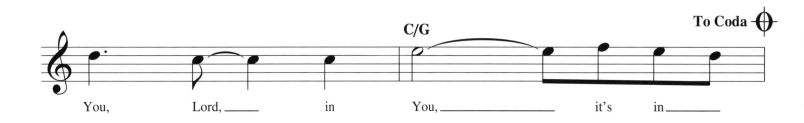

You. My You. I will praise You ___ with

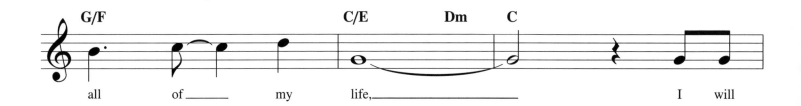

all of ___ my life, _____ I will

praise You ____ with all of ____ my strength. ____

____ With all of ____ my life, with

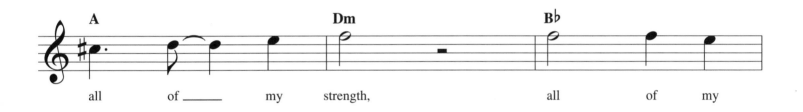

all of ____ my strength, all of my

D.S. al Coda
(with repeat)

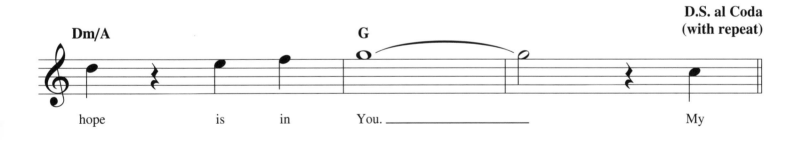

hope is in You. ____ My

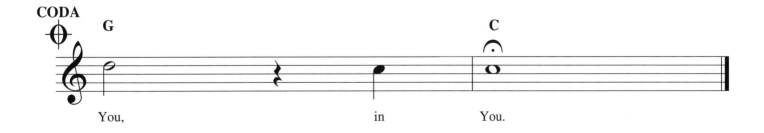

You, in You.

MY REDEEMER LIVES

Words and Music by
REUBEN MORGAN

High energy

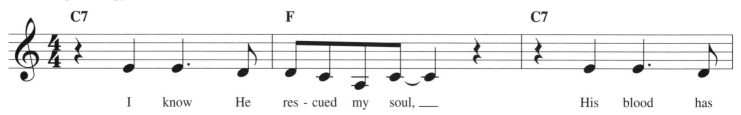

I know He res - cued my soul, ___ His blood has

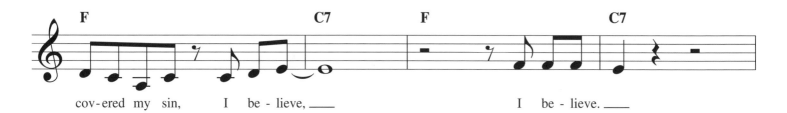

cov-ered my sin, I be - lieve, ___ I be - lieve. ___

My shame He's tak-en a - way, ___ My pain is

healed in His name. I be - lieve, ___ I be - lieve. ___

___ I'll raise a ban - ner

'cause my Lord has con-quered the grave! My Re - deem - er lives! ___

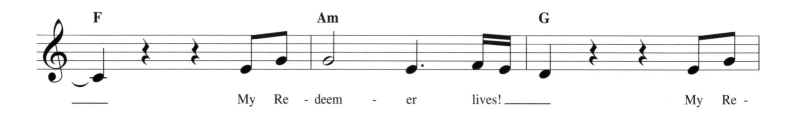

___ My Re - deem - er lives! ___ My Re -

deem - er lives! _____ My Re - deem - er lives! _____

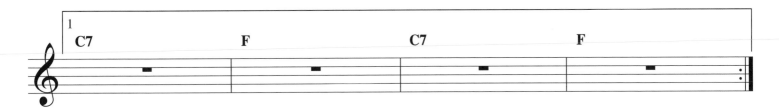

1
C7   F   C7   F

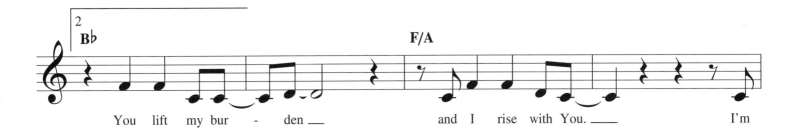

2
B♭   F/A

You lift my bur - den _____ and I rise with You. _____ I'm

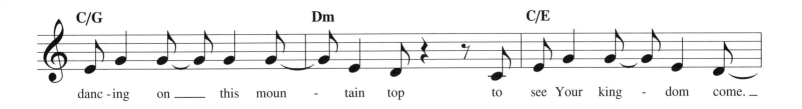

C/G   Dm   C/E

danc -ing on _____ this moun - tain top to see Your king - dom come. _

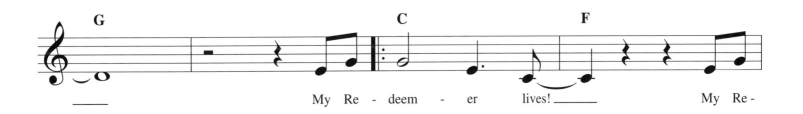

G   C   F

_____ My Re - deem - er lives! _____ My Re -

Am   G   C   F

deem - er lives! _____ My Re - deem - er lives! _____ My Re -

Am   Repeat as desired / G   Song ending / G   C

deem - er lives! _____ My Re - _____

MY TRIBUTE

Words and Music by
ANDRAÉ CROUCH

With expression

How _____ can I say thanks for the things You have done for me?

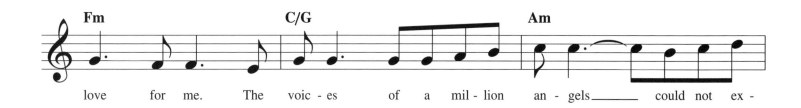

Things _____ so un - de - served, yet You give _____ to prove Your

love for me. The voic - es of a mil - lion an - gels _____ could not ex -

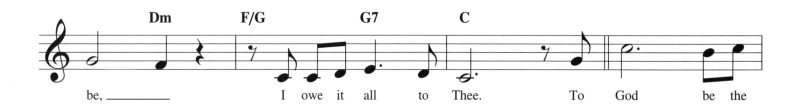

press _____ my grat - i - tude. All that I am and ev - er hope to

be, _____ I owe it all to Thee. To God be the

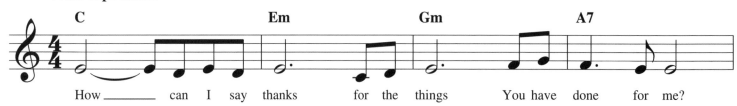

glo - ry, to God be the glo - ry, to God be the

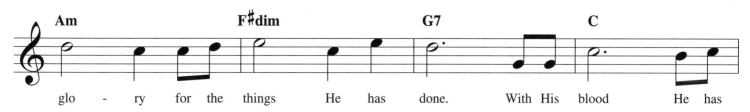

glo - ry for the things He has done. With His blood He has

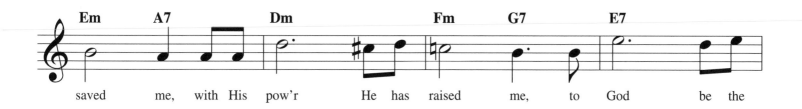

saved me, with His pow'r He has raised me, to God be the

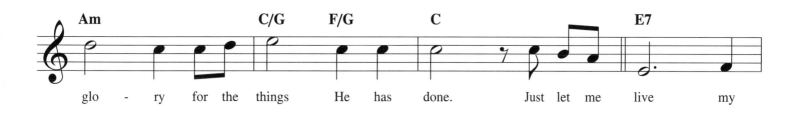

glo - ry for the things He has done. Just let me live my

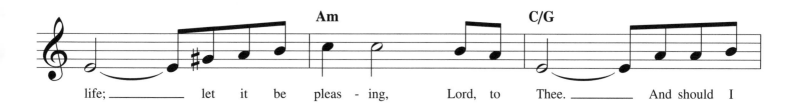

life; _____ let it be pleas - ing, Lord, to Thee. _____ And should I

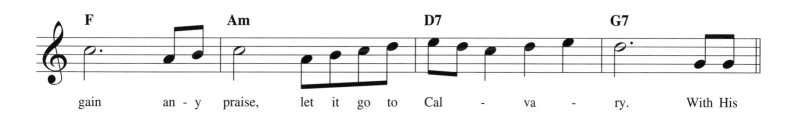

gain an - y praise, let it go to Cal - va - ry. With His

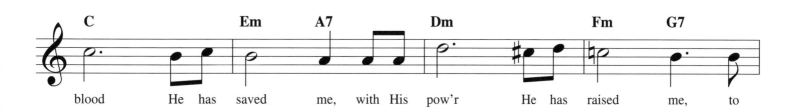

blood He has saved me, with His pow'r He has raised me, to

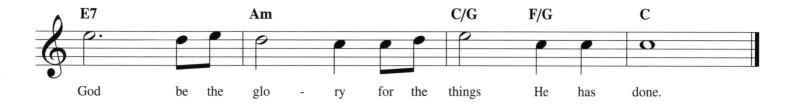

God be the glo - ry for the things He has done.

OH LORD, YOU'RE BEAUTIFUL

Words and Music by
KEITH GREEN

Oh (3.) Lord, You're beau - ti - ful. Your face is all I
(2.) Lord, please light the fire that once burned bright and

seek, for when Your eyes are on this child, Your
clear. Re - place the lamp of my first love that

grace a - bounds to me. Oh
burns with ho - ly fear. I want to take Your Word and

shine it all a - round, but first help me just to live it,

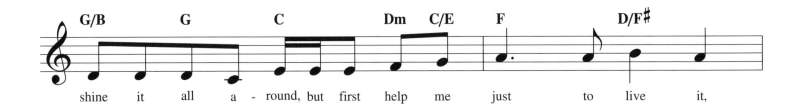

Lord. And when I'm do - ing well, help me to nev - er seek a crown, for my re -

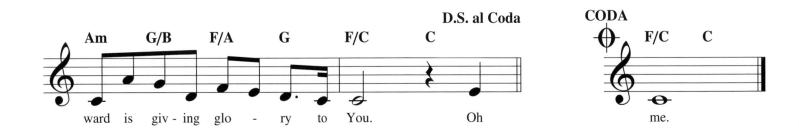

ward is giv - ing glo - ry to You. Oh   me.

OPEN OUR EYES

Words and Music by
BOB CULL

Prayerfully

O - pen our eyes, Lord, _____ we

want to see Je - sus, _____ to

reach out and touch Him, _____ and

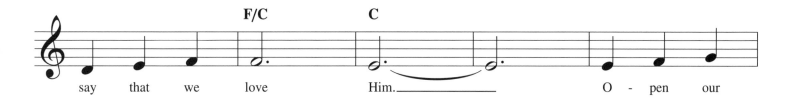

say that we love Him. _____ O - pen our

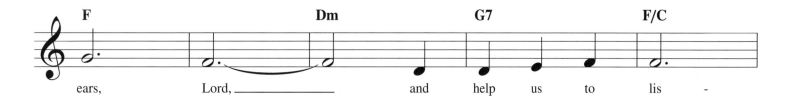

ears, Lord, _____ and help us to lis -

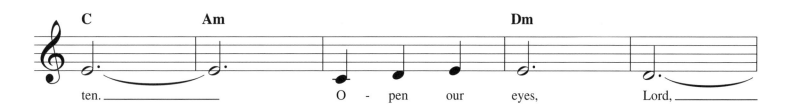

ten. _____ O - pen our eyes, Lord, _____

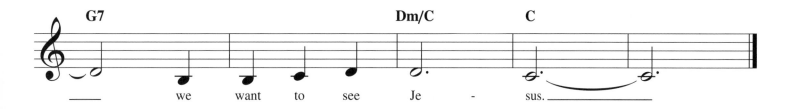

_____ we want to see Je - sus. _____

ONCE AGAIN

Words and Music by
MATT REDMAN

Reflectively

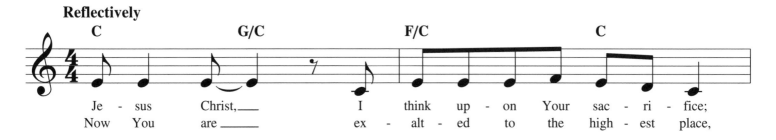

Je - sus Christ,___ I think up - on Your sac - ri - fice;
Now You are ___ ex - alt - ed to the high - est place,

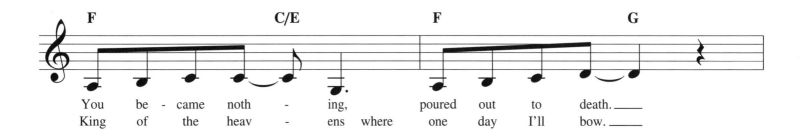

You be - came noth - ing, poured out to death.___
King of the heav - ens where one day I'll bow.___

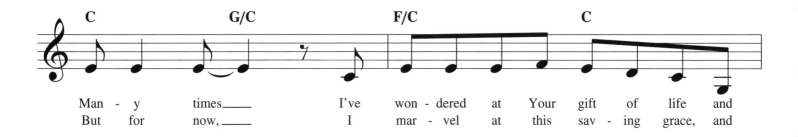

Man - y times___ I've won - dered at Your gift of life and
But for now,___ I mar - vel at this sav - ing grace, and

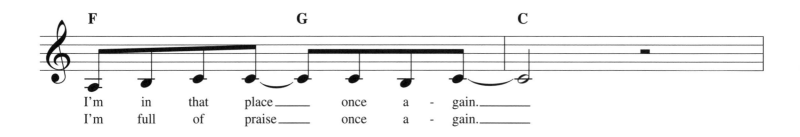

I'm in that place___ once a - gain.___
I'm full of praise___ once a - gain.___

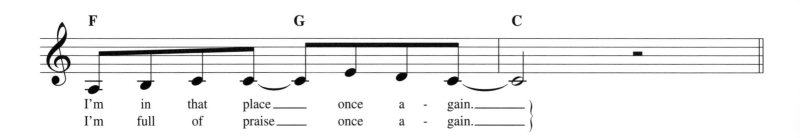

I'm in that place___ once a - gain.___
I'm full of praise___ once a - gain.___

Once a-gain I look up-on the cross where You died,____ I'm

hum-bled by Your mer-cy and I'm bro-ken in-side.____

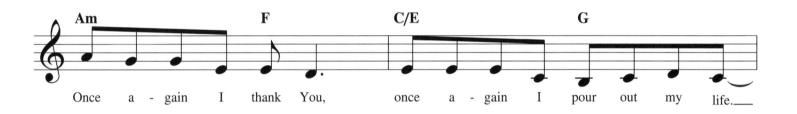

Once a-gain I thank You, once a-gain I pour out my life.____

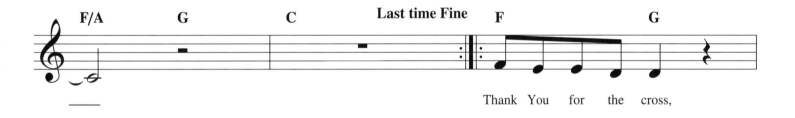

____ Thank You for the cross,

thank You for the cross, thank You for the cross, my

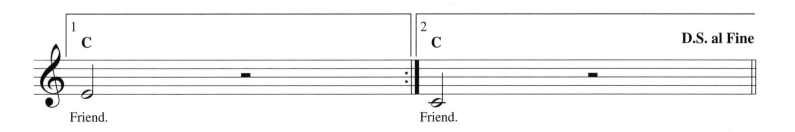

Friend.   Friend.

OPEN THE EYES OF MY HEART

Words and Music by
PAUL BALOCHE

O - pen the eyes of my heart, Lord,

o - pen the eyes of my heart. I want to

see You, I want to see You.

To see You high and lift - ed up, —

— shin - ing in the light of Your glo -

-ry. _____ Pour out _____ Your pow'r and love _____

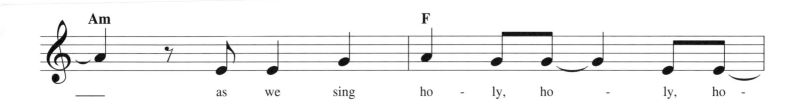

_____ as we sing ho - ly, ho - ly, ho -

-ly. _____ Ho - ly, ho - ly, ho - ly. _____

Ho - ly, ho - ly, ho - ly. _____ Ho - ly, ho - ly, ho -

-ly. _____ I want ___ to see You. _____

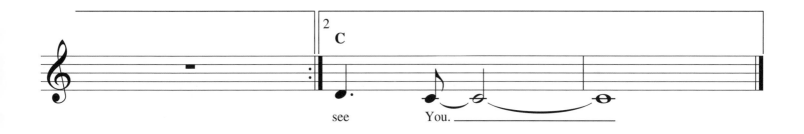

see You. _____

THE POTTER'S HAND

Words and Music by
DARLENE ZSCHECH

Moderately

Beau-ti-ful Lord, __ won-der-ful Sav - ior, I know for sure, __

all of my days __ are held in Your hand, __ craft-ed in-to __ Your

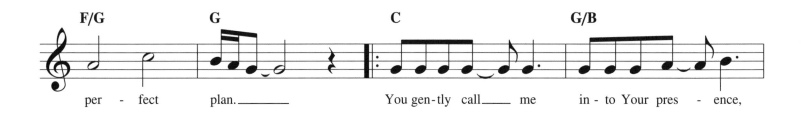

per - fect plan. __ You gen-tly call __ me in-to Your pres - ence,

guid-ing me by __ Your Ho-ly Spir - it. Teach me, dear Lord, __ to live

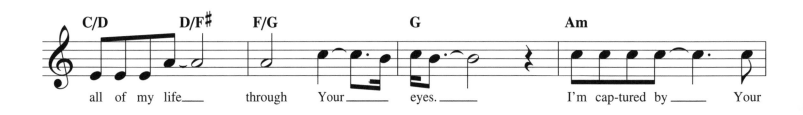

all of my life __ through Your __ eyes. __ I'm cap-tured by __ Your

Ho-ly call - ing. Set me a-part, __ I know You're draw-ing me __

113

to Your-self. Lead me, Lord, I pray.

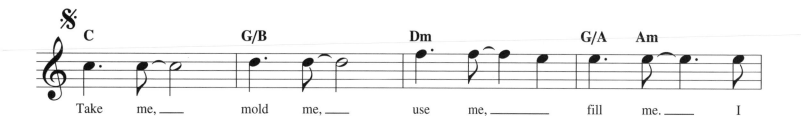

Take me, mold me, use me, fill me. I

give my life to the Pot - ter's hand. Call me,

guide me, lead me, walk be - side me. I give my life

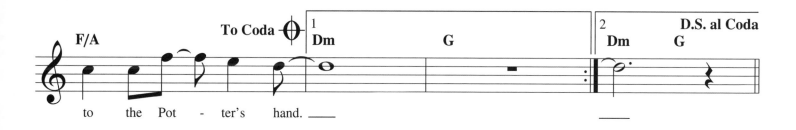

to the Pot - ter's hand.

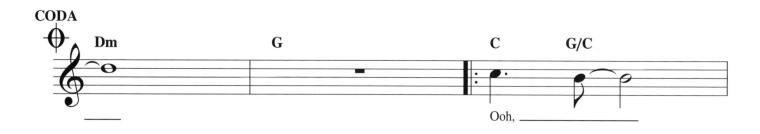

Ooh,

ooh, ooh.

THE POWER OF YOUR LOVE

Words and Music by
GEOFF BULLOCK

Moderately

Lord, I come to You, ___ let my heart be ___ changed, ___ re - newed, ___
Lord, un - veil my eyes, ___ let me see You ___ face ___ to face, ___

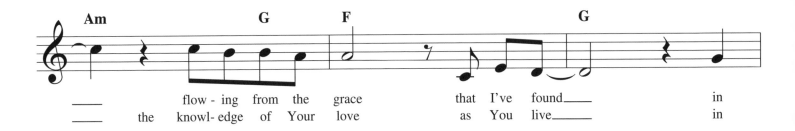

___ flow - ing from the grace that I've found ___ in
___ the knowl- edge of Your love as You live ___ in

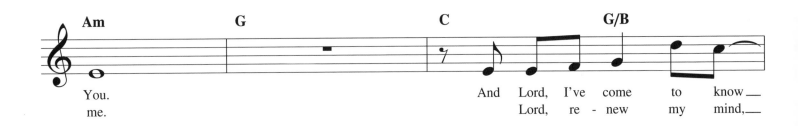

You. And Lord, I've come to know ___
me. Lord, re - new my mind, ___

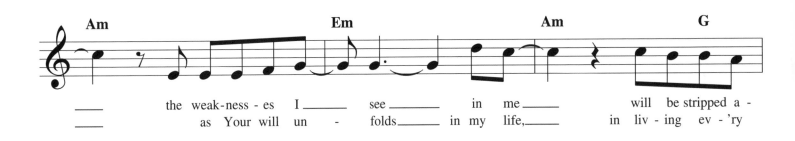

___ the weak-ness - es I ___ see ___ in me ___ will be stripped a -
___ as Your will un - folds ___ in my life, ___ in liv - ing ev - 'ry

way by the pow'r of Your love. ___
day in the pow'r of Your love. ___

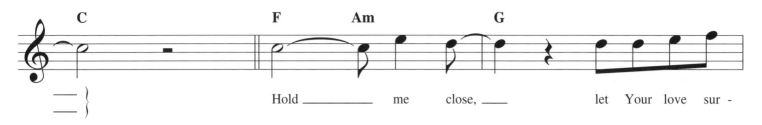

C   F   Am   G

Hold _____ me close, ____ let Your love sur-

Dm/C   C   F   Am

round _____ me. ____ Bring _____ me near, __

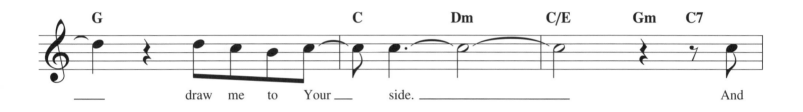

G   C   Dm   C/E   Gm   C7

____ draw me to Your __ side. _____ And

F   Am   G   Dm/C

as _____ I wait, ____ I'll rise up like the ea - gle, __

C   G/B   Am   G

____ and I will soar with You; Your Spir - it leads me

F   F/G   F/C   C

on in the pow'r of Your love. _____

REFINER'S FIRE

Words and Music by
BRIAN DOERKSEN

Moderately, with expression

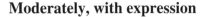

Pu - ri - fy____ my heart,____ let me be as gold and
Pu - ri - fy____ my heart,____ cleanse me from with - in and

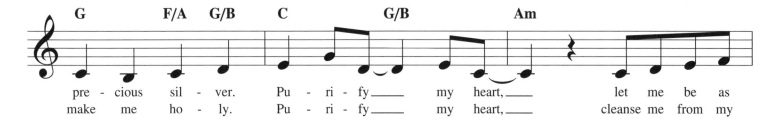

pre - cious sil - ver.   Pu - ri - fy____ my heart,____ let me be as
make me ho - ly.   Pu - ri - fy____ my heart,____ cleanse me from my

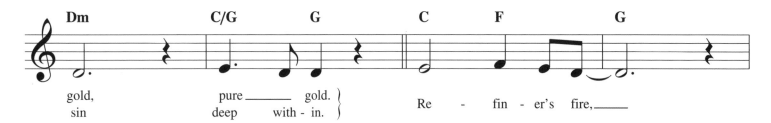

gold,   pure____ gold.   }
sin   deep with - in.   }   Re - fin - er's fire,____

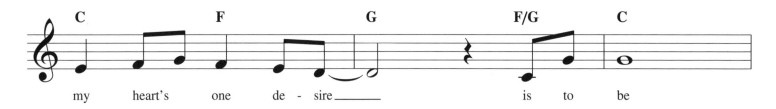

my heart's one de - sire____ is to be

ho - ly,   set____ a - part____ for You,____ Lord.   I choose to

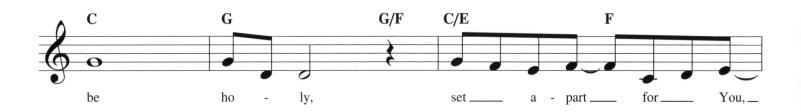

be ho - ly,   set____ a - part____ for____ You,____

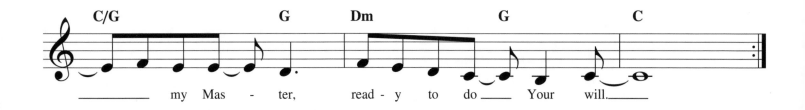

_____ my Mas - ter,   read - y to do____ Your will.____

SANCTUARY

Words and Music by JOHN THOMPSON
and RANDY SCRUGGS

Moderately slow

Lord, pre - pare me ____ to be a sanc - tu - ar - y, pure and

ho - ly, tried and true. ____ With thanks - giv - ing, I'll be a

liv - ing sanc - tu - ar - y for ____ You. Lord, pre -

pare me ____ to be a sanc - tu - ar - y, pure and

ho - ly, tried and true. ____ With thanks - giv - ing, I'll be a

liv - ing sanc - tu - ar - y for ____ You.

RISE UP AND PRAISE HIM

Words and Music by PAUL BALOCHE
and GARY SADLER

Let the heav-ens re-joice, ____ let the earth __ be __ glad. __

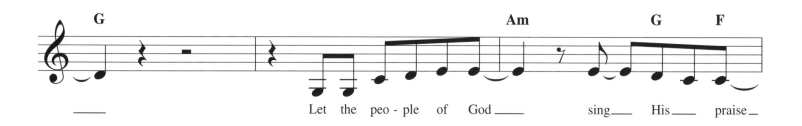

__ Let the peo-ple of God __ sing __ His __ praise

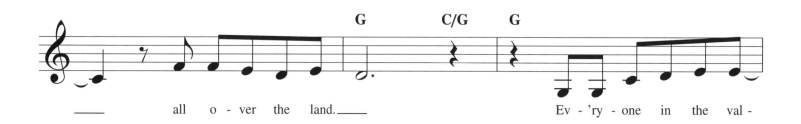

__ all o-ver the land. __ Ev-'ry-one in the val-

-ley come and lift __ your __ voice. __

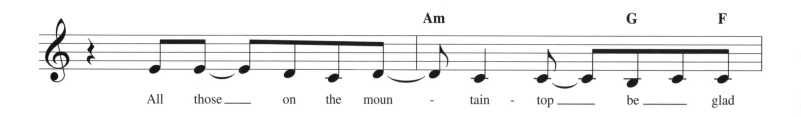

All those __ on the moun-tain-top __ be __ glad

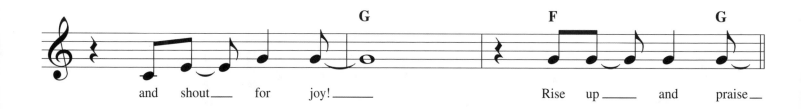

and shout __ for joy! __ Rise up __ and praise __

Him, ____ He de - serves _ our ___ love. ___

Rise up ___ and praise ___ Him, ___ wor - ship the Ho -

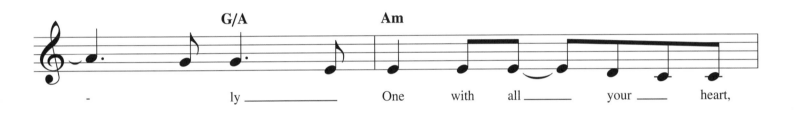

- ly _____ One with all ____ your ___ heart,

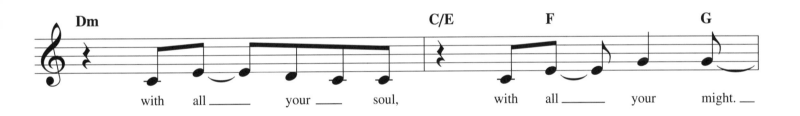

with all ____ your _ soul, with all ____ your _ might. __

___ Rise up ___ and praise ___ Him! ___

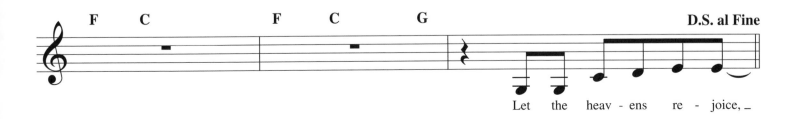

Let the heav - ens re - joice, _

SEEK YE FIRST

Words and Music by
KAREN LAFFERTY

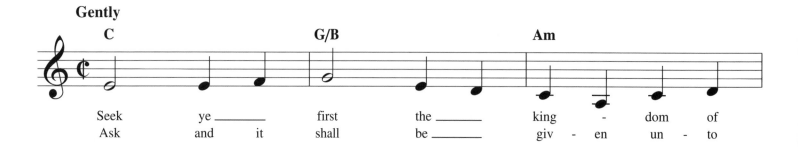

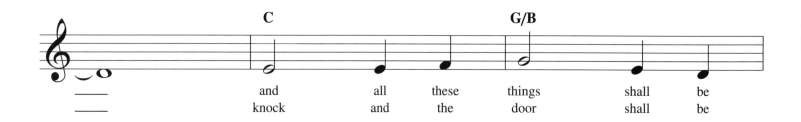

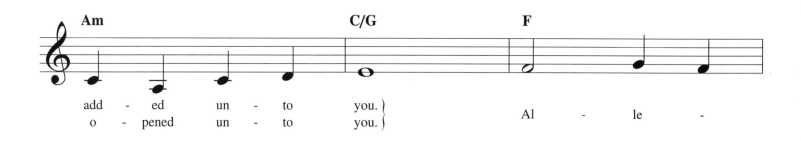

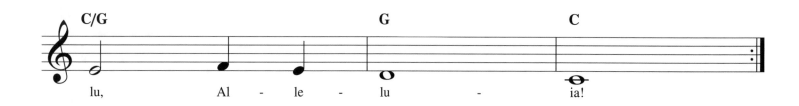

SHINE ON US

Words and Music by MICHAEL W. SMITH
and DEBBIE SMITH

Expressively

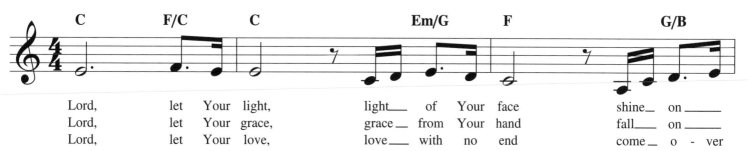

Lord,   let Your light,   light___ of Your face   shine__ on _____
Lord,   let Your grace,   grace__ from Your hand   fall__ on _____
Lord,   let Your love,   love__ with no end   come_ o - ver

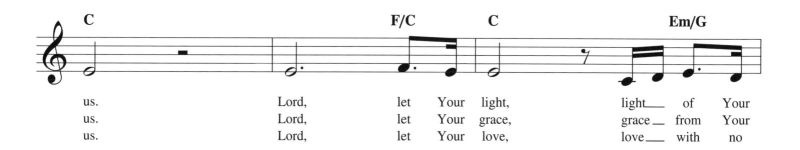

us.   Lord,   let Your light,   light___ of Your
us.   Lord,   let Your grace,   grace__ from Your
us.   Lord,   let Your love,   love__ with no

face   shine__ on _____ us,
hand   fall__ on _____ us,   that we may be
end   come_ o - ver us,

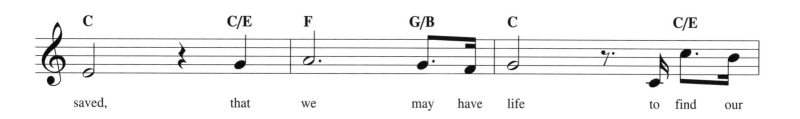

saved,   that we may have life   to find our

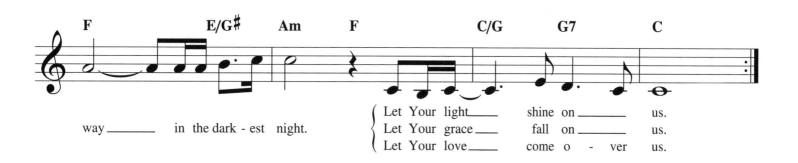

way _____ in the dark - est night.   Let Your light____ shine on _____ us.
Let Your grace ____ fall on _____ us.
Let Your love____ come o - ver us.

SHINE, JESUS, SHINE

Words and Music by
GRAHAM KENDRICK

With excitement

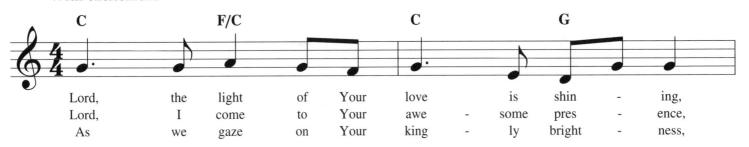

Lord, the light of Your love is shin - ing,
Lord, I come to Your awe - some pres - ence,
As we gaze on Your king - ly bright - ness,

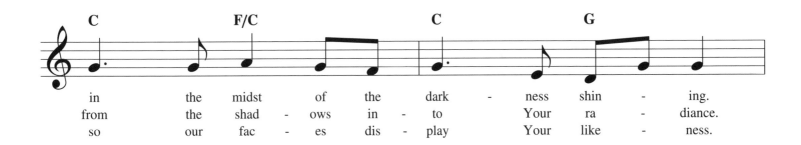

in the midst of the dark - ness shin - ing.
from the shad - ows in - to Your ra - diance.
so our fac - es dis - play Your like - ness.

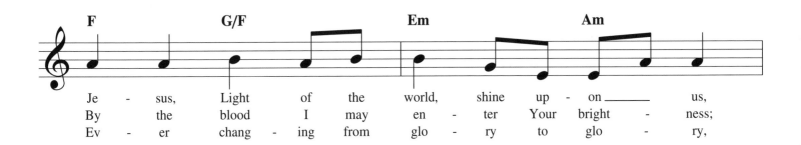

Je - sus, Light of the world, shine up - on us,
By the blood I may en - ter Your bright - ness;
Ev - er chang - ing from glo - ry to glo - ry,

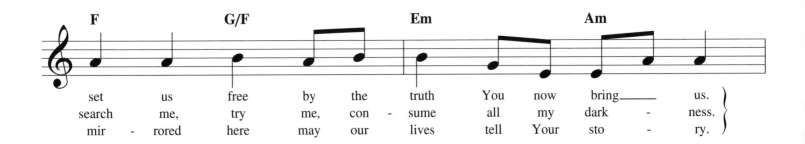

set us free by the truth You now bring us.
search me, try me, con - sume all my dark - ness.
mir - rored here may our lives tell Your sto - ry.

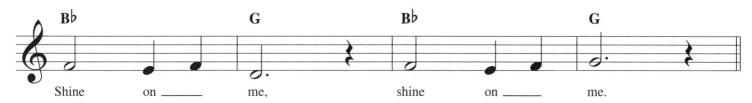

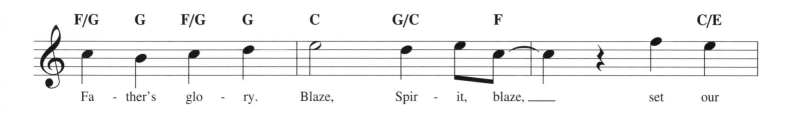

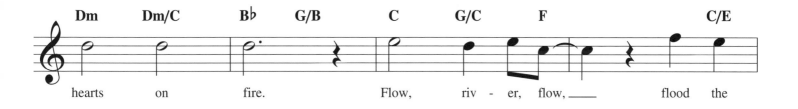

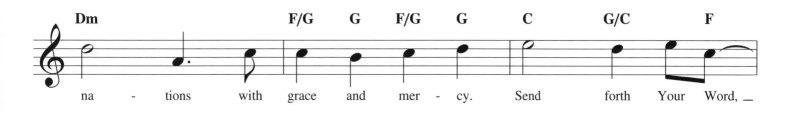

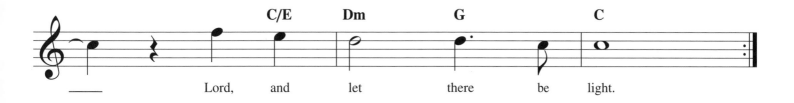

SHOUT TO THE LORD

Words and Music by
DARLENE ZSCHECH

Worshipfully

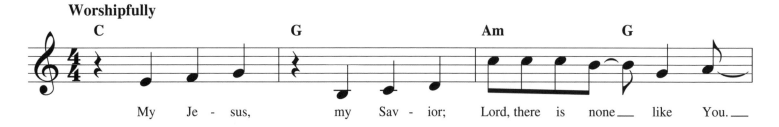

My   Je - sus,   my   Sav - ior;   Lord, there is none___ like   You.___

___   All of my days___   I want to praise___   the won - ders of Your

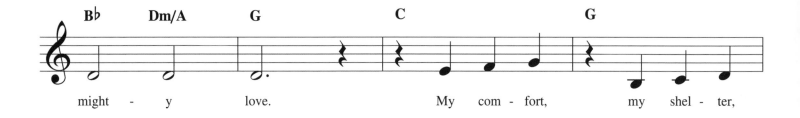

might - y   love.   My com - fort,   my shel - ter,

tow - er of ref - uge and strength;___   let ev - 'ry breath,___   all that I am,___

___   nev - er cease to wor - ship You.

Shout to the Lord, ___ all the earth, ___ let us sing ___

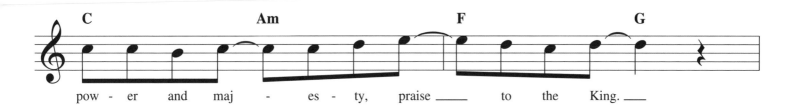

pow - er and maj - es - ty, praise ___ to the King. ___

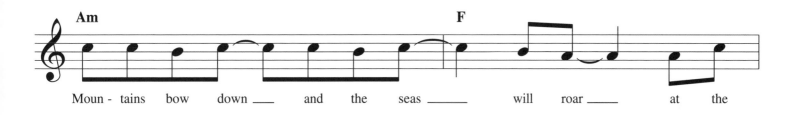

Moun - tains bow down ___ and the seas ___ will roar ___ at the

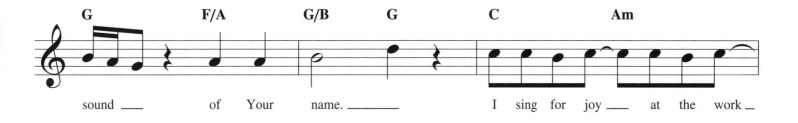

sound ___ of Your name. ___ I sing for joy ___ at the work ___

___ of Your hand. _ For - ev - er I'll love ___ You, for - ev - er I'll stand.

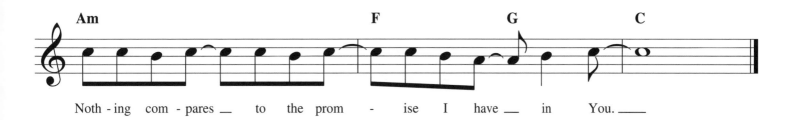

Noth - ing com - pares ___ to the prom - ise I have ___ in You. ___

SHOUT TO THE NORTH

Words and Music by
MARTIN SMITH

Moderately slow, in 2

Men of faith, rise up and sing of the great and glo - rious
wom - en of the truth; stand and sing to bro - ken
church with bro - ken wings; fill this place with songs a -

King. You are strong when you feel weak; in your bro - ken - ness, com -
hearts. Who can know the heal - ing pow'r of our awe - some King of
gain, of our God who reigns on high. By His grace a - gain we'll

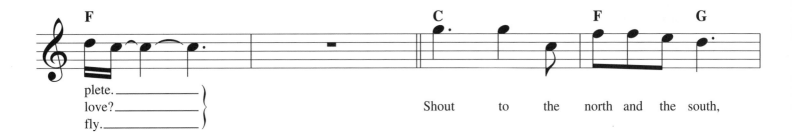

plete._____
love?_____
fly._____

Shout to the north and the south,

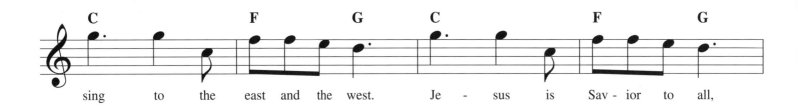

sing to the east and the west. Je - sus is Sav - ior to all,

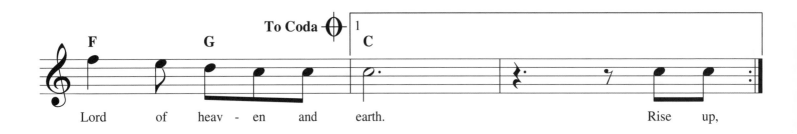

To Coda ⊕ 1

Lord of heav - en and earth. Rise up,

2

earth. We've been through fi - re, we've been through rain,

Am .... **F** .... **Am**

we've been re - fined by the pow'r of His name. We've fall - en deep - er

F .... **G**

in love with You; You've burned the truth on our lips. _____

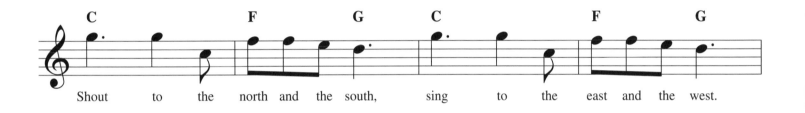

C .... **F** ... **G** ... **C** .... **F** ... **G**

Shout to the north and the south, sing to the east and the west.

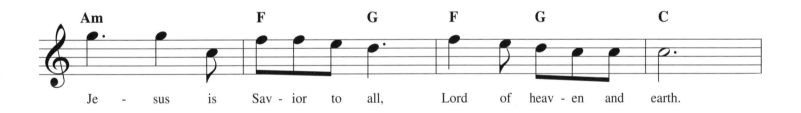

Am .... **F** ... **G** ... **F** ... **G** .... **C**

Je - sus is Sav - ior to all, Lord of heav - en and earth.

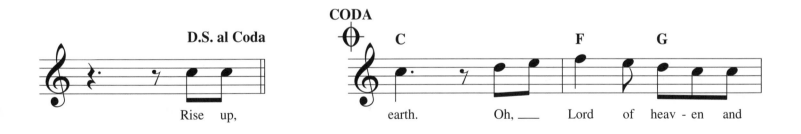

D.S. al Coda .... **CODA** ... **C** .... **F** ... **G**

Rise up, ... earth. Oh, ___ Lord of heav - en and

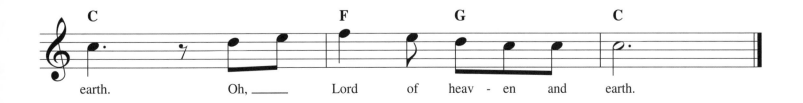

C .... **F** ... **G** .... **C**

earth. Oh, _____ Lord of heav - en and earth.

SONG OF LOVE

Words and Music by REBECCA ST. JAMES,
MATT BRONLEEWE and JEREMY ASH

Moderately

Je - sus, ___ King of my heart. ___ Fa - ther, ___ my

peace and my light. ___ Spir - it, ___ the

joy of my soul ___ You are. ___

Je - sus, ___ to You none com - pare. ___ Fa - ther, ___ I
Je - sus, ___ You saved my soul. ___ I'll thank You ___

rest in Your care. ___ Spir - it, ___ the hope for my heart ___ You are. ___
for - ev - er - more. ___ Je - sus, ___ the love of my life ___ You are. ___

The heav - ens ___ de -

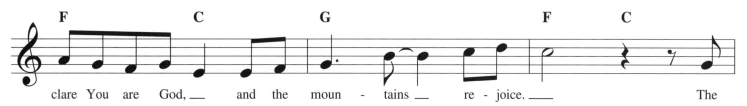

clare You are God, __ and the moun - tains __ re - joice. __ The

o - ceans _____ cry "Al - le - lu - ia" _____ as we wor - ship __ You, Lord, __

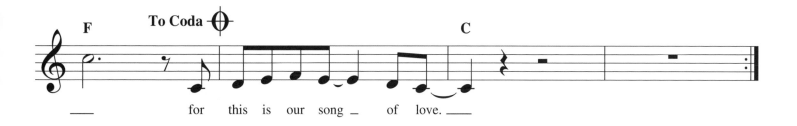

__ for this is our song _ of love. __

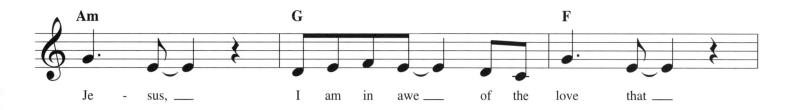

Je - sus, __ I am in awe __ of the love that __

You have shown. Je - sus, __ how pre - cious You are ___ to me, __

__ to me. _____ The

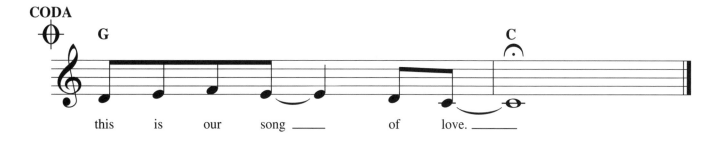

this is our song _____ of love. _____

SPIRIT OF THE LIVING GOD

Words and Music by DANIEL IVERSON
and LOWELL ALEXANDER

Gently

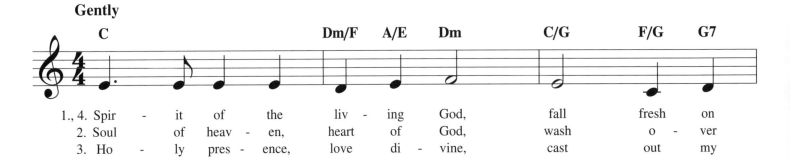

1., 4. Spir - it of the liv - ing God, fall fresh on
2. Soul of heav - en, heart of God, wash o - ver
3. Ho - ly pres - ence, love di - vine, cast out my

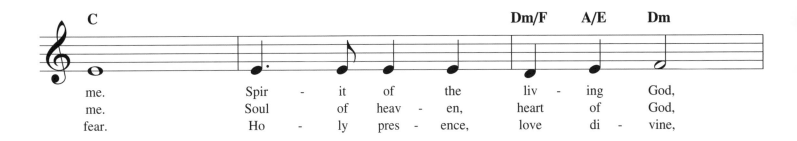

me. Spir - it of the liv - ing God,
me. Soul of heav - en, heart of God,
fear. Ho - ly pres - ence, love di - vine,

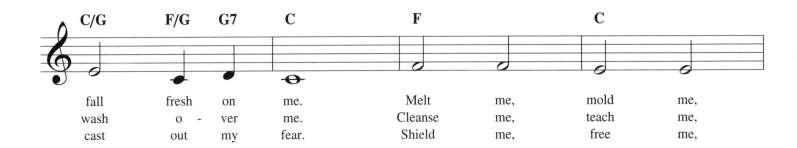

fall fresh on me. Melt me, mold me,
wash o - ver me. Cleanse me, teach me,
cast out my fear. Shield me, free me,

fill me, use me. ____ Spir - it of the
hold me, reach me. ____ Soul of heav - en,
call me, lead me. ____ Ho - ly pres - ence,

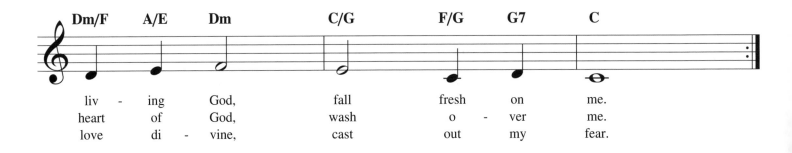

liv - ing God, fall fresh on me.
heart of God, wash o - ver me.
love di - vine, cast out my fear.

STEP BY STEP

Words and Music by
DAVID STRASSER "BEAKER"

Moderately fast

O God, You are my ___ God, and

I will ev-er praise ___ You. O God, You are my ___

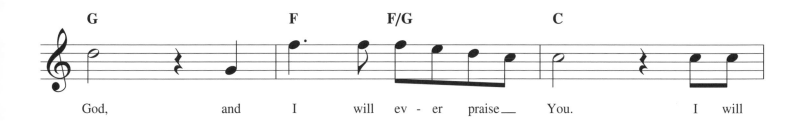

God, and I will ev-er praise ___ You. I will

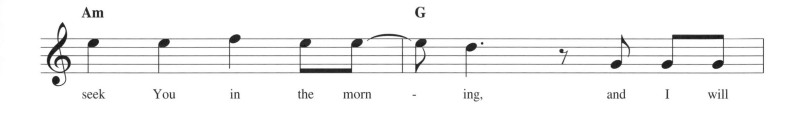

seek You in the morn - ing, and I will

learn to walk in Your ___ ways. ___ And step by step You'll lead ___

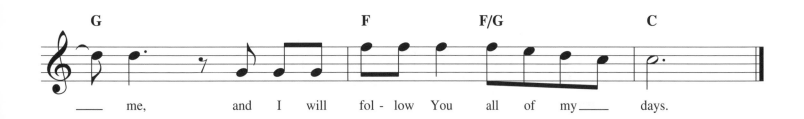

___ me, and I will fol-low You all of my ___ days.

THAT'S WHY WE PRAISE HIM

Words and Music by
TOMMY WALKER

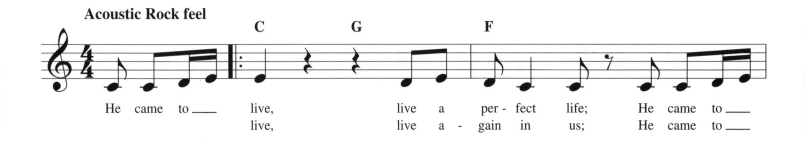

He came to ___ live, live a per-fect life; He came to ___
live, live a-gain in us; He came to ___

be the Liv-ing Word, our Light. He came to die so we'd be
be our con-qu'ring King and Friend. He came to heal and show the

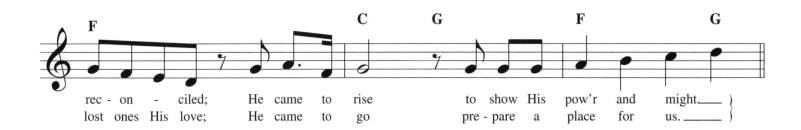

rec-on-ciled; He came to rise to show His pow'r and might.___ }
lost ones His love; He came to go pre-pare a place for us. ___ }

That's why we praise ___ Him, that's why we sing. ___

That's why we of-fer Him our ev-'ry-thing. ___

That's why we bow ___ down and wor - ship this King, ___ 'cause He

gave His ___ ev - 'ry - thing, 'cause He

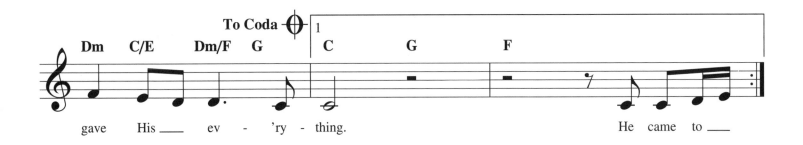

gave His ___ ev - 'ry - thing. He came to ___

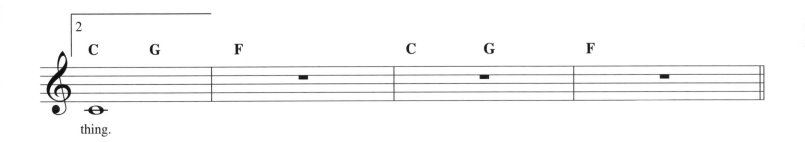

thing.

Hal - le, hal - le - lu - jah. Hal - le,

hal - le - lu - jah.

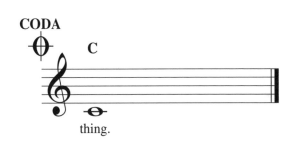

thing.

THERE IS A REDEEMER

Words and Music by
MELODY GREEN

Moderately

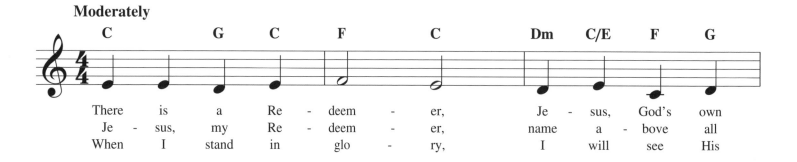

There is a Re - deem - er, Je - sus, God's own
Je - sus, my Re - deem - er, name a - bove all
When I stand in glo - ry, I will see His

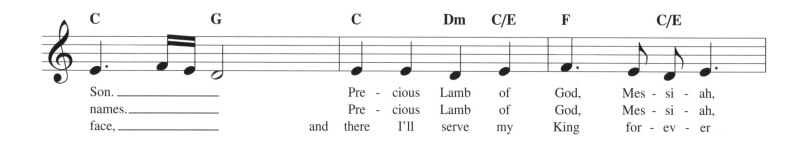

Son. _____ Pre - cious Lamb of God, Mes - si - ah,
names. _____ Pre - cious Lamb of God, Mes - si - ah,
face, _____ and there I'll serve my King for - ev - er

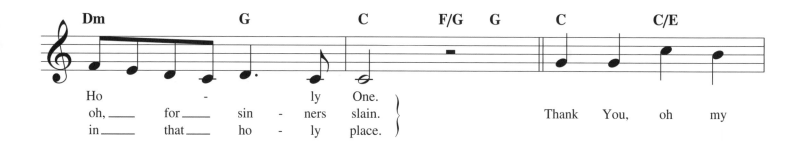

Ho - ly One.
oh, _____ for _____ sin - ners slain. Thank You, oh my
in _____ that _____ ho - ly place.

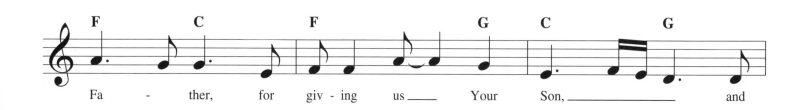

Fa - ther, for - giv - ing us _____ Your Son, _____ and

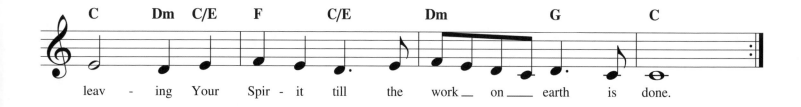

leav - ing Your Spir - it till the work _____ on _____ earth is done.

THIS IS THE DAY

By LES GARRETT

Joyfully

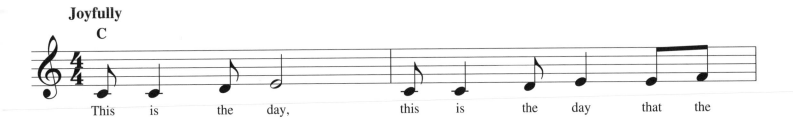

This is the day, this is the day that the

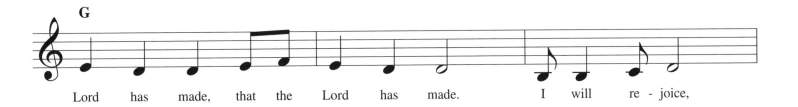

Lord has made, that the Lord has made. I will re - joice,

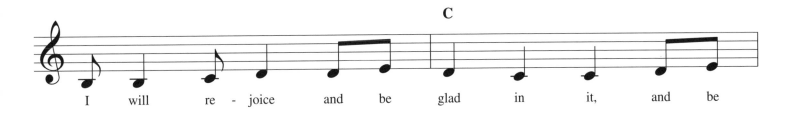

I will re - joice and be glad in it, and be

glad in it. This is the day that the Lord has ___ made;

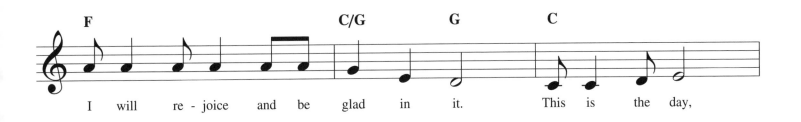

I will re - joice and be glad in it. This is the day,

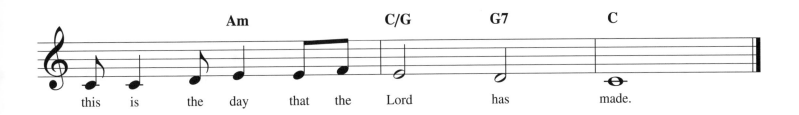

this is the day that the Lord has made.

THERE IS NONE LIKE YOU

Words and Music by
LENNY LeBLANC

Worshipfully

There is none like___ You. No one else___ can touch my

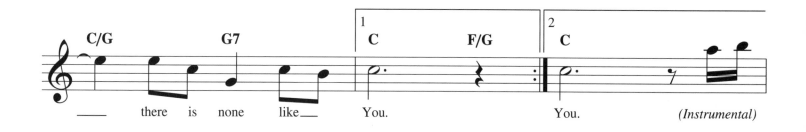

heart like You do. ___ I could search___ for all e - ter - ni - ty long___ and find___

___ there is none like___ You. You. *(Instrumental)*

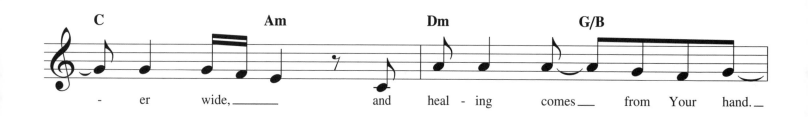

Your mer - cy flows___ like a riv-

- er wide,_____ and heal - ing comes___ from Your hand. ___

___ Suf - fer - ing___ chil - dren are safe___

C   **Am**   **Dm**   **F/C**

___ in Your arms; _____ there is none like

G/B   **F/A**   **G/B**   **C**   **G/B**   **F/A**   **C/G**

You.   There is none like ___ You.

F   **C/E**   **Dm**   **G**

No one else ___ can touch my heart like You do. ___

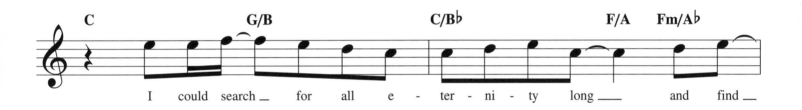

C   **G/B**   **C/B♭**   **F/A**   **Fm/A♭**

I could search ___ for all e - ter - ni - ty long ___ and find ___

C/G   **G7**   **C**   **F/A**   **G/B**   **C**   **G/B**

___ there is none like ___ You.   I could search ___ for all e -

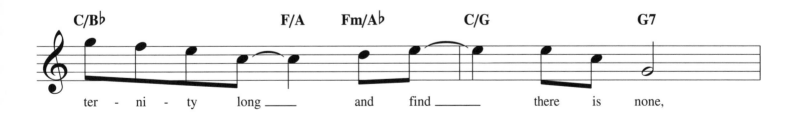

C/B♭   **F/A**   **Fm/A♭**   **C/G**   **G7**

ter - ni - ty long ___ and find _____ there is none,

C/G   **G7**   **C/G**   **G7**   **C**

there is none,   there is none like ___ You.

TRADING MY SORROWS

Words and Music by
DARRELL EVANS

Moderately fast Rock

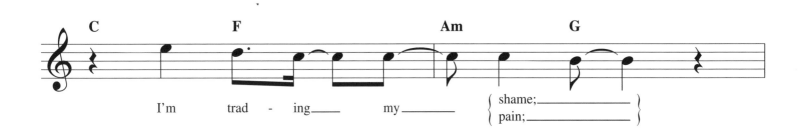

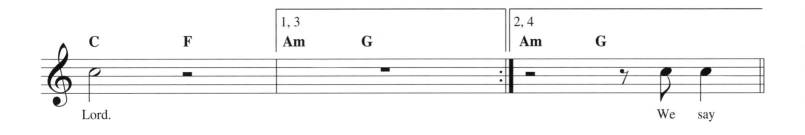

To Coda ⊕

yes, yes, Lord. __ Yes, Lord, yes, Lord, yes, yes, Lord, A - men. __

__ I am pressed __ but not crushed, per - se -

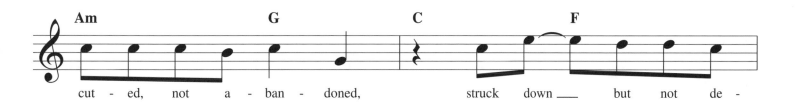

cut - ed, not a - ban - doned, struck down __ but not de -

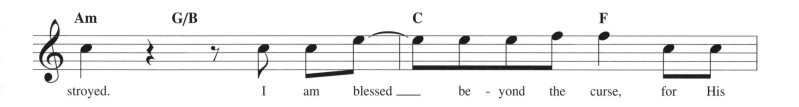

stroyed. I am blessed __ be - yond the curse, for His

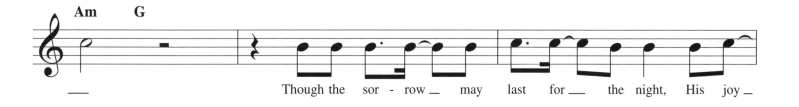

prom - ise will en - dure, that His joy is gon - na be my strength. __

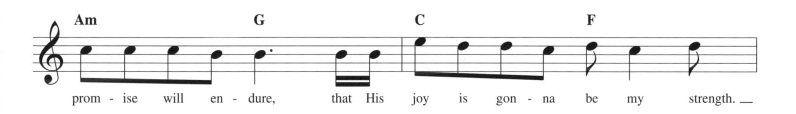

__ Though the sor - row __ may last for __ the night, His joy __

D.C. al Coda
(with repeat)

CODA

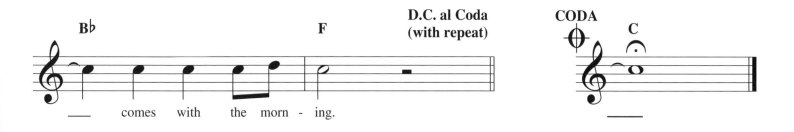

__ comes with the morn - ing. __

WE BOW DOWN

Words and Music by
TWILA PARIS

Flowing, in one

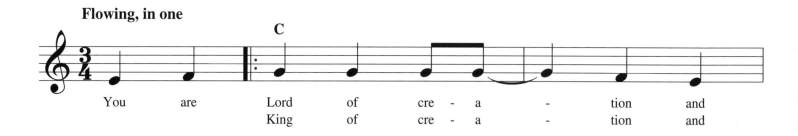

You are Lord of cre - a - tion and
King of cre - a - tion and

Lord of my ____ life, Lord of the land ___
King of my ____ life, King of the land ___

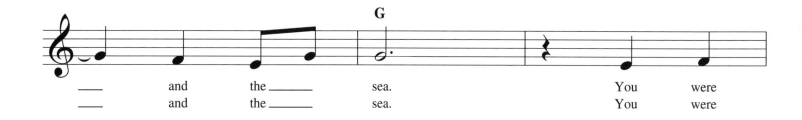

___ and the ____ sea. You were
___ and the ____ sea. You were

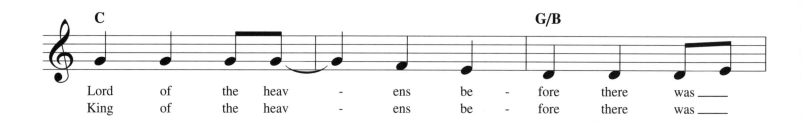

Lord of the heav - ens be - fore there was ___
King of the heav - ens be - fore there was ___

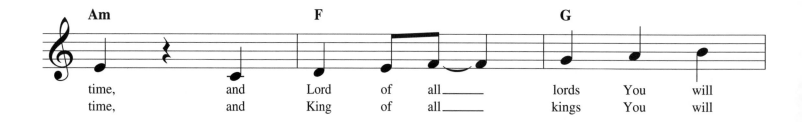

time, and Lord of all ____ lords You will
time, and King of all ____ kings You will

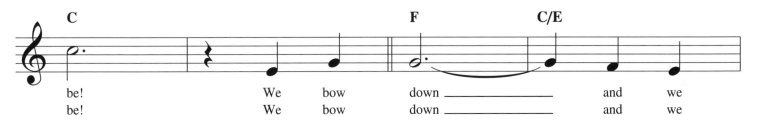

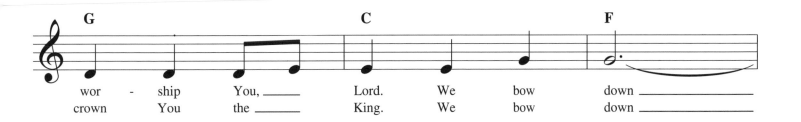

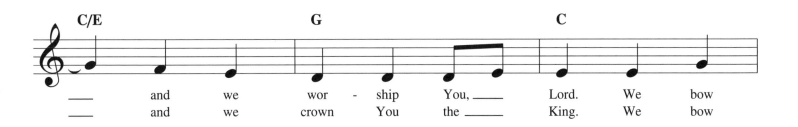

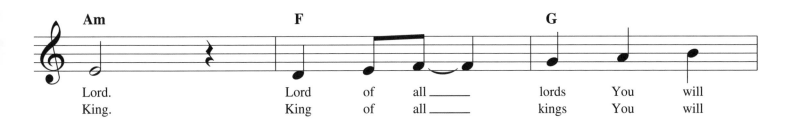

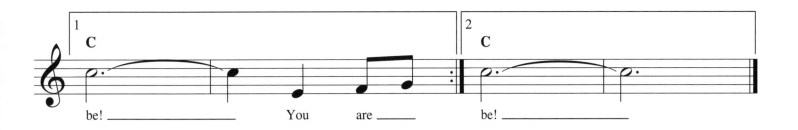

WE FALL DOWN

Words and Music by
CHRIS TOMLIN

Worshipfully

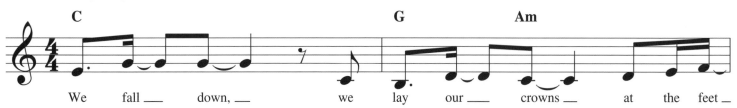

We fall down, we lay our crowns at the feet

of Je - sus, the great - ness of

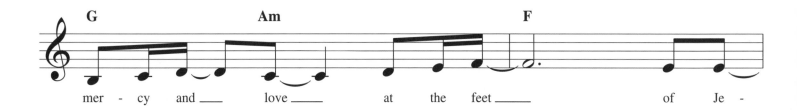

mer - cy and love at the feet of Je -

- sus. And we cry, "Ho - ly, ho - ly, ho -

- ly," and we cry, "Ho - ly, ho - ly, ho -

- ly," and we cry, "Ho - ly, ho - ly, ho -

- ly is the Lamb."

WE WILL GLORIFY

Words and Music by
TWILA PARIS

Moderately

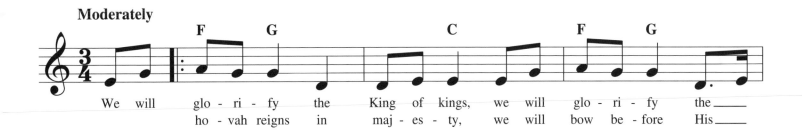

We will glo - ri - fy the King of kings, we will glo - ri - fy the ____
ho - vah reigns in maj - es - ty, we will bow be - fore His ____

Lamb. We will glo - ri - fy the Lord of lords, who ____ is the great I ____
throne. We will wor - ship Him in right - eous - ness, we will wor - ship Him a -

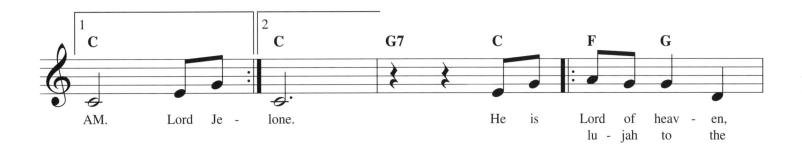

1. AM. Lord Je - lone.
2. He is Lord of heav - en,
   lu - jah to the

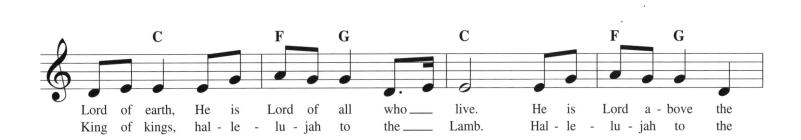

Lord of earth, He is Lord of all who ____ live. He is Lord a - bove the
King of kings, hal - le - lu - jah to the ____ Lamb. Hal - le - lu - jah to the

u - ni - verse, all ____ praise to Him we ____ give. Hal - le -
Lord of lords, who ____ is the great I ____   AM.

WE WILL WORSHIP THE LAMB OF GLORY

Words and Music by
DENNIS JERNIGAN

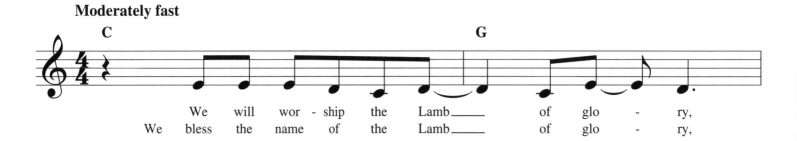

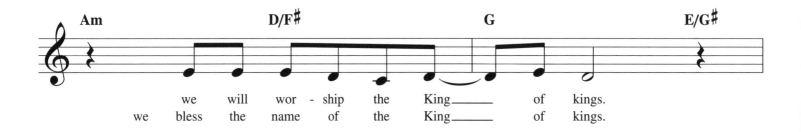

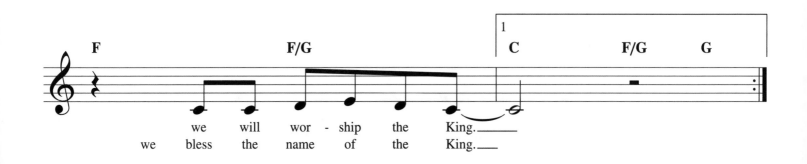

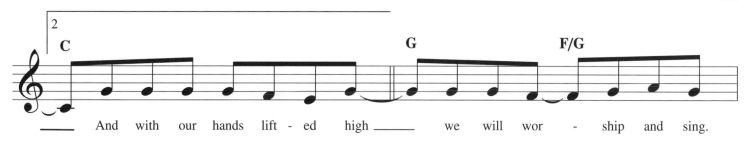

And with our hands lift - ed high _____ we will wor - ship and sing.

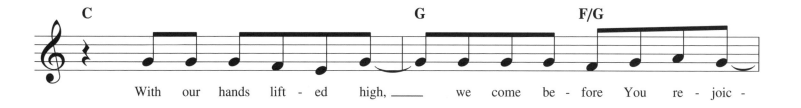

With our hands lift - ed high, _____ we come be - fore You re - joic -

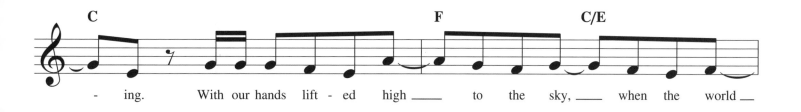

- ing. With our hands lift - ed high _____ to the sky, _____ when the world _____

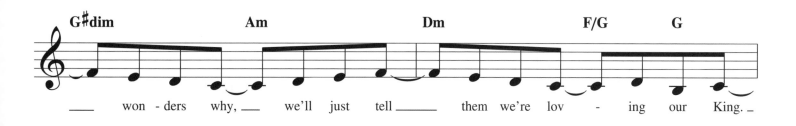

_____ won - ders why, ___ we'll just tell _____ them we're lov - ing our King. _____

We'll just tell _____ them we're lov - ing our King. _____

THE WONDERFUL CROSS

Words and Music by JESSE REEVES,
CHRIS TOMLIN and J.D. WALT

With awe

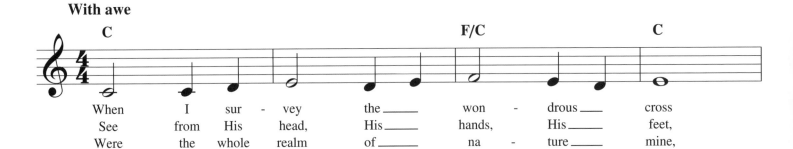

When   I   sur - vey   the ____ won - drous ____ cross
See   from   His   head,   His ____ hands,   His ____ feet,
Were   the   whole   realm   of ____ na - ture ____ mine,

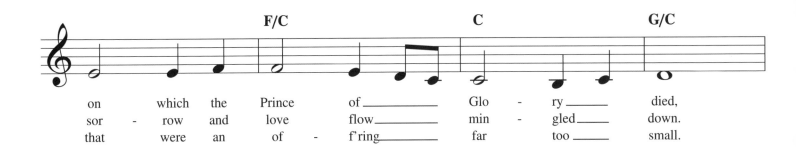

on   which   the   Prince   of _____ Glo - ry ____ died,
sor - row   and   love   flow_____ min - gled ____ down.
that   were   an   of - f'ring_____ far   too ____ small.

my   rich - est   gain   I ____ count   but ____ loss,
Did   e'er   such   love   and ____ sor - row ____ meet,
Love   so   a - maz - ing, ____ so   di - vine,

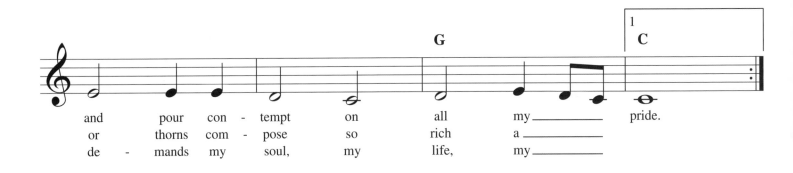

1.
and   pour   con - tempt   on   all   my _____ pride.
or   thorns   com - pose   so   rich   a _____
de - mands   my   soul,   my   life,   my _____

2, 3
crown? }
all. }   O   the   won - der - ful   cross, ____ O   the

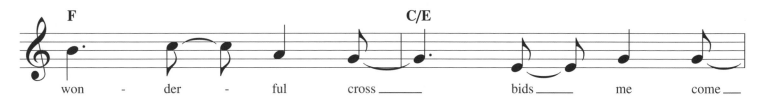

won - der - ful cross _____ bids _____ me come _____

_____ and die _____ and find _____ that _____ I _____ may tru -

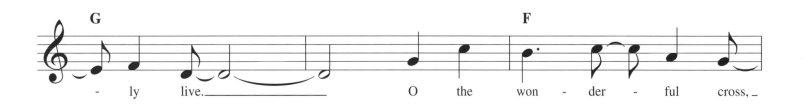

- ly live. _____ O the won - der - ful cross, _

_____ O the won - der - ful cross; ___ all ___ who gath -

- er here _____ by grace _____ draw _____ near _____ and bless _

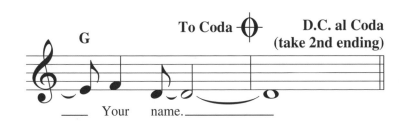

_____ Your name. _____

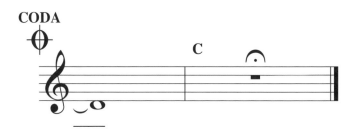

WORTHY IS THE LAMB

Words and Music by
DARLENE ZSCHECH

Thank You for the cross,_____ Lord._____ Thank You for the

price You paid.___ Bear-ing all my sin and shame,___ in

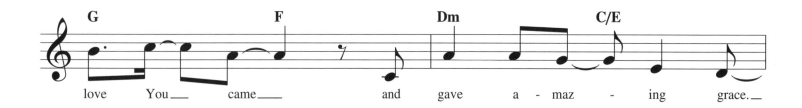

love You___ came___ and gave a-maz-ing grace.___

_____ Thank You for this love,_____ Lord._____ Thank You for the

nail-pierced hands.___ Washed me in Your cleans-ing flow,___ now

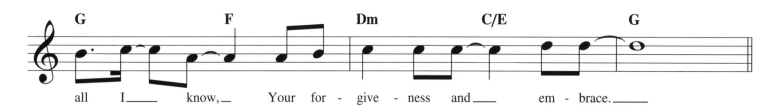

all I___ know,___ Your for-give-ness and___ em-brace.___

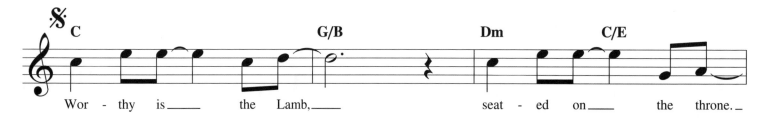

Wor-thy is___ the Lamb,___ seat-ed on___ the throne.___

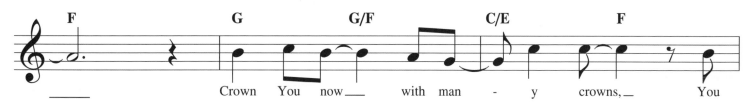

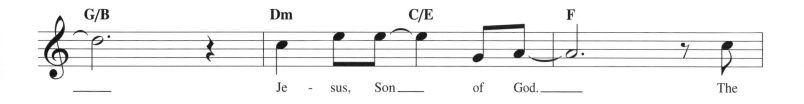

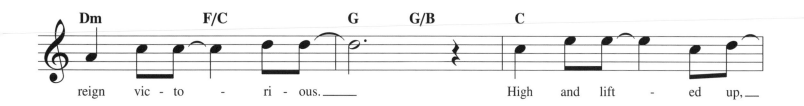

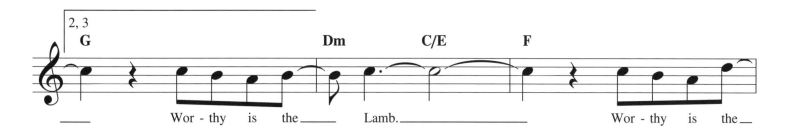

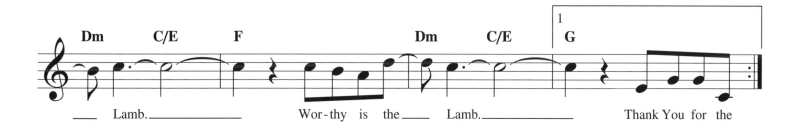

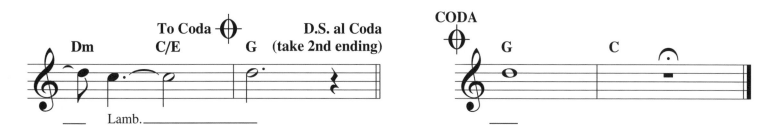

WORTHY OF WORSHIP

Words by TERRY YORK
Music by MARK BLANKENSHIP

Flowing

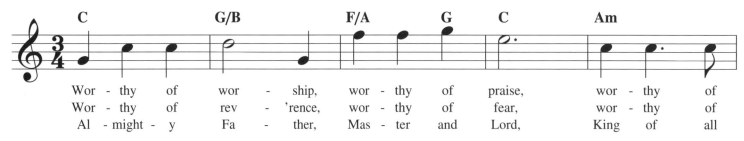

Wor - thy of wor - ship, wor - thy of praise, wor - thy of
Wor - thy of rev - 'rence, wor - thy of fear, wor - thy of
Al - might - y Fa - ther, Mas - ter and Lord, King of all

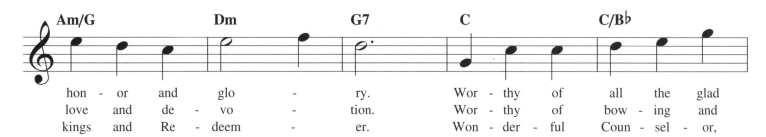

hon - or and glo - ry. Wor - thy of all the glad
love and de - vo - tion. Wor - thy of bow - ing and
kings and Re - deem - er. Won - der - ful Coun - sel - or,

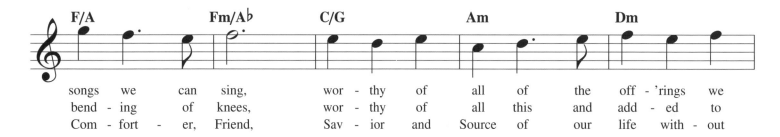

songs we can sing, wor - thy of all of the off - 'rings we
bend - ing of knees, wor - thy of all this and add - ed to
Com - fort - er, Friend, Sav - ior and Source of our life with - out

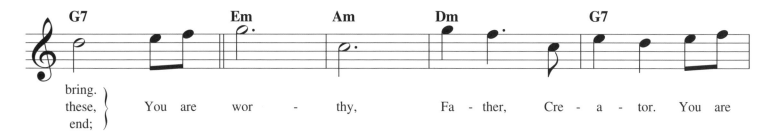

bring. }
these, } You are wor - thy, Fa - ther, Cre - a - tor. You are
end; }

wor - thy, Sav - ior, Sus - tain - er. You are

wor - thy, wor - thy and won - der - ful,

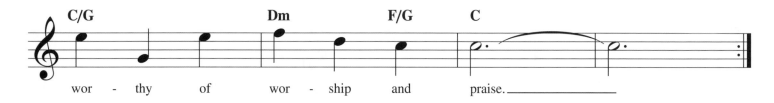

wor - thy of wor - ship and praise.

WORTHY, YOU ARE WORTHY

Words and Music by
DON MOEN

Moderately

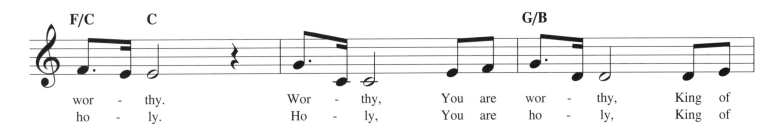

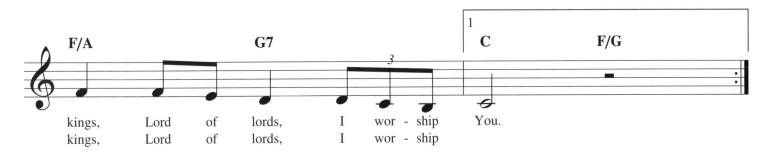

YOU ARE MY KING
(Amazing Love)

Words and Music by
BILLY JAMES FOOTE

Moderately slow

I'm for-giv-en be - cause You were for-sak - en.

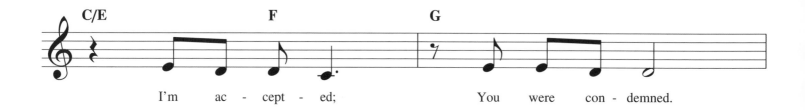

I'm ac-cept - ed; You were con-demned.

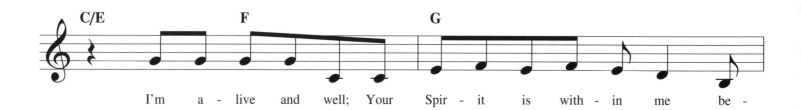

I'm a-live and well; Your Spir-it is with-in me be -

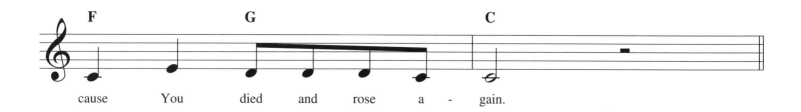

cause You died and rose a - gain.

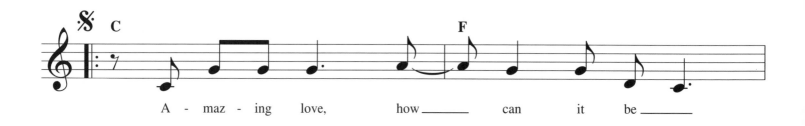

A - maz-ing love, how _____ can it be _____

that You, my King, would die ___ for me? A - maz-ing love, I ___

To Coda ⊕

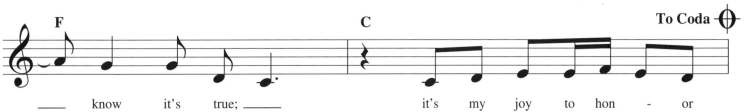

know it's true; ____ it's my joy to hon - or

You. You. In all I ____ do, ___ I hon - or

You. You are __ my ____ King.

You are __ my ____ King. Je - sus, You are __ my _

D.S. al Coda
(with repeat)

___ King. Je - sus, You are __ my ____ King.

CODA ⊕

You. In all I ____ do, ___ I hon - or You.

YOU'RE WORTHY OF MY PRAISE

Words and Music by
DAVID RUIS

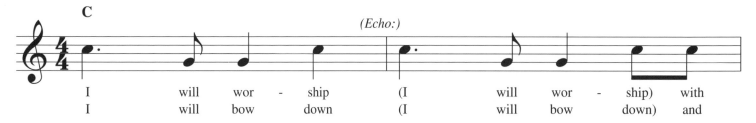

Moderately

(Echo:)

I   will   wor - ship   (I   will   wor - ship)   with
I   will   bow   down   (I   will   bow - down)   and

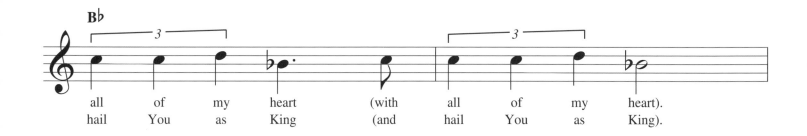

all   of   my   heart   (with   all   of   my   heart).
hail   You   as   King   (and   hail   You   as   King).

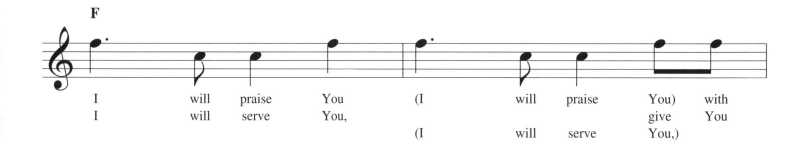

I   will   praise   You   (I   will   praise   You)   with
I   will   serve   You,   (I   will   serve   You,)   give   You

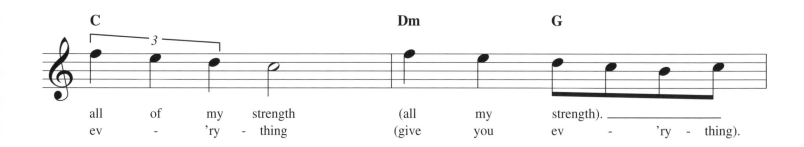

all   of   my   strength   (all   my   strength). _____
ev - 'ry - thing   (give   you   ev - 'ry - thing).

I   will   seek   You   (I   will   seek   You)   all   of   my   days
I   will   lift   up   (I   will   lift   up)   my   eyes   to   Your   throne   (my

(all of my days). I will fol - low (I will fol - low)
eyes to Your throne). I will trust You (I will trust You),

all of Your ways (all Your ways).
trust of You a - lone (trust in You a - lone).

I will give ___ You all my wor - ship,

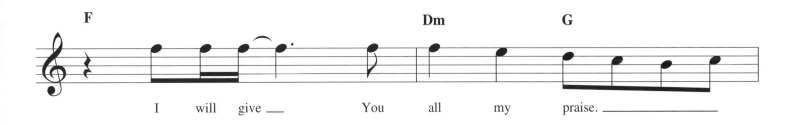

I will give ___ You all my praise. ___

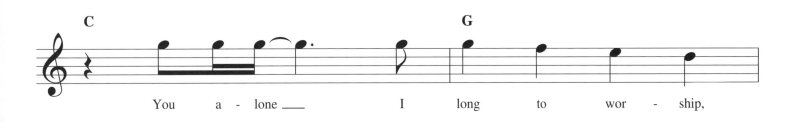

You a - lone ___ I long to wor - ship,

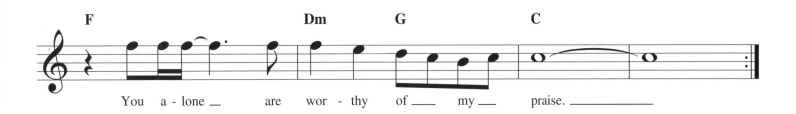

You a - lone ___ are wor - thy of ___ my ___ praise. ___

YOU ARE MY ALL IN ALL

By DENNIS JERNIGAN

Moderately

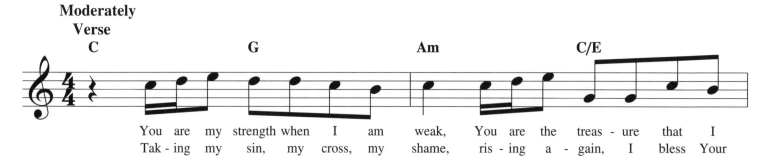

Verse

You are my strength when I am weak, You are the treas - ure that I
Tak - ing my sin, my cross, my shame, ris - ing a - gain, I bless Your

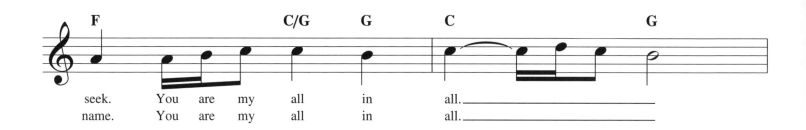

seek. You are my all in all.
name. You are my all in all.

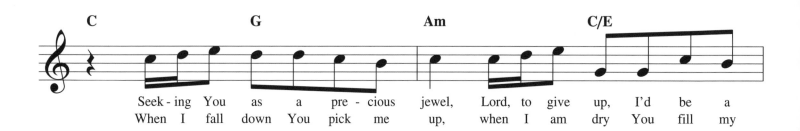

Seek - ing You as a pre - cious jewel, Lord, to give up, I'd be a
When I fall down You pick me up, when I am dry You fill my

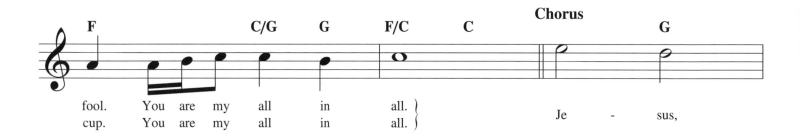

fool. You are my all in all.
cup. You are my all in all.

Chorus

Je - sus,

Lamb of God, wor - thy is Your name!

Je - sus, Lamb of God, Wor - thy is Your name!

Note: The Verse and Chorus may be sung simultaneously.

CHORD SPELLER

C chords

C	C–E–G
Cm	C–E♭–G
C7	C–E–G–B♭
Cdim	C–E♭–G♭
C+	C–E–G♯

C♯ or D♭ chords

C♯	C♯–F–G♯
C♯m	C♯–E–G♯
C♯7	C♯–F–G♯–B
C♯dim	C♯–E–G
C♯+	C♯–F–A

D chords

D	D–F♯–A
Dm	D–F–A
D7	D–F♯–A–C
Ddim	D–F–A♭
D+	D–F♯–A♯

E♭ chords

E♭	E♭–G–B♭
E♭m	E♭–G♭–B♭
E♭7	E♭–G–B♭–D♭
E♭dim	E♭–G♭–A
E♭+	E♭–G–B

E chords

E	E–G♯–B
Em	E–G–B
E7	E–G♯–B–D
Edim	E–G–B♭
E+	E–G♯–C

F chords

F	F–A–C
Fm	F–A♭–C
F7	F–A–C–E♭
Fdim	F–A♭–B
F+	F–A–C♯

F♯ or G♭ chords

F♯	F♯–A♯–C♯
F♯m	F♯–A–C♯
F♯7	F♯–A♯–C♯–E
F♯dim	F♯–A–C
F♯+	F♯–A♯–D

G chords

G	G–B–D
Gm	G–B♭–D
G7	G–B–D–F
Gdim	G–B♭–D♭
G+	G–B–D♯

G♯ or A♭ chords

A♭	A♭–C–E♭
A♭m	A♭–B–E♭
A♭7	A♭–C–E♭–G♭
A♭dim	A♭–B–D
A♭+	A♭–C–E

A chords

A	A–C♯–E
Am	A–C–E
A7	A–C♯–E–G
Adim	A–C–E♭
A+	A–C♯–F

B♭ chords

B♭	B♭–D–F
B♭m	B♭–D♭–F
B♭7	B♭–D–F–A♭
B♭dim	B♭–D♭–E
B♭+	B♭–D–F♯

B chords

B	B–D♯–F♯
Bm	B–D–F♯
B7	B–D♯–F♯–A
Bdim	B–D–F
B+	B–D♯–G

Important Note: A slash chord (C/E, G/B) tells you that a certain bass note is to be played under a particular harmony. In the case of C/E, the chord is C and the bass note is E.

THE EASY FAKE BOOK SERIES

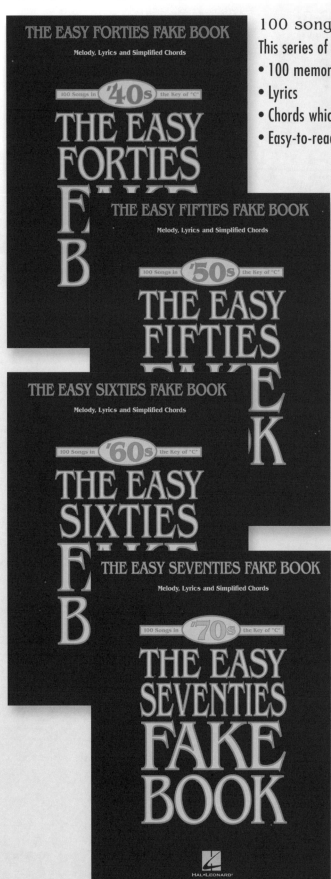

100 songs from your favorite decades of music

This series of beginning fake books for players new to "faking" includes:
- 100 memorable songs, all in the key of C
- Lyrics
- Chords which have been simplified, but remain true to each tune
- Easy-to-read, large music notation

THE EASY FORTIES FAKE BOOK

This '40s edition includes: Ac-cent-tchu-ate the Positive • The Anniversary Waltz • Be Careful, It's My Heart • Bésame Mucho (Kiss Me Much) • Bewitched • Boogie Woogie Bugle Boy • Come Rain or Come Shine • Don't Get Around Much Anymore • Easy Street • Frenesí • Harlem Nocturne • Have I Told You Lately That I Love You • How High the Moon • I Got It Bad and That Ain't Good • I'll Remember April • I'm Beginning to See the Light • It Could Happen to You • Java Jive • Love Letters • Mairzy Doats • Moonlight in Vermont • A Nightingale Sang in Berkeley Square • On a Slow Boat to China • Sentimental Journey • Stella by Starlight • The Surrey with the Fringe on Top • Tangerine • You'd Be So Nice to Come Home To • You're Nobody 'til Somebody Loves You • and dozens more.
00240252 Melody/Lyrics/Chords..$19.95

THE EASY FIFTIES FAKE BOOK

Includes: All I Have to Do Is Dream • At the Hop • Beyond the Sea • Blueberry Hill • Chantilly Lace • Don't Be Cruel (To a Heart That's True) • Dream Lover • Earth Angel • Great Balls of Fire • Heartbreak Hotel • Jambalaya (On the Bayou) • Kansas City • La Bamba • Love and Marriage • Love Me Tender • Magic Moments • Mister Sandman • Mona Lisa • Peggy Sue • Put Your Head on My Shoulder • Que Sera, Sera (Whatever Will Be, Will Be) • Rock Around the Clock • Sea of Love • Sh-Boom (Life Could Be a Dream) • Sixteen Candles • Smoke Gets in Your Eyes • Splish Splash • Tennessee Waltz • Unchained Melody • You Belong to Me • Your Cheatin' Heart • and dozens more.
00240255 Melody/Lyrics/Chords..$19.95

THE EASY SIXTIES FAKE BOOK

100 songs from the '60s: Along Comes Mary • Baby Love • Barbara Ann • Born to Be Wild • Brown Eyed Girl • California Girls • Call Me • Dancing in the Street • Do Wah Diddy Diddy • Do You Know the Way to San Jose • The Girl from Ipanema • Good Vibrations • A Groovy Kind of Love • Happy Together • Hey Jude • I Can't Help Myself (Sugar Pie, Honey Bunch) • I Heard It Through the Grapevine • Leader of the Pack • Leaving on a Jet Plane • Louie, Louie • Magic Carpet Ride • Moon River • Respect • (Sittin' On) The Dock of the Bay • Soul Man • Strangers in the Night • Sweet Caroline • Turn! Turn! Turn! • The Twist • Yesterday • and more.
00240253 Melody/Lyrics/Chords..$19.95

THE EASY SEVENTIES FAKE BOOK

Songs from the '70s edition include: Ain't No Mountain High Enough • American Pie • Angie • Baby, I Love Your Way • Bad, Bad Leroy Brown • The Boys Are Back in Town • Come Sail Away • Crocodile Rock • Drift Away • Fame • Free Bird • Honesty • I Will Survive • I'll Never Love This Way Again • Joy to the World • Let It Be • Rainy Days and Mondays • Reeling in the Years • She Believes in Me • Stayin' Alive • Take a Chance on Me • Take Me Home, Country Roads • We Are the Champions • Wonderful Tonight • Y.M.C.A. • You Are So Beautiful • You've Got a Friend • dozens more.
00240256 Melody/Lyrics/Chords..$19.95

Visit Hal Leonard online at **www.halleonard.com** for complete songlists and more.

FOR MORE INFORMATION, SEE YOUR LOCAL MUSIC DEALER, OR WRITE TO:

HAL•LEONARD®
CORPORATION
7777 W. BLUEMOUND RD. P.O. BOX 13819 MILWAUKEE, WI 53213

Prices, contents and availability subject to change without notice.

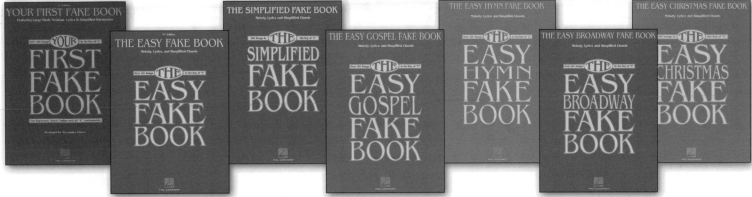

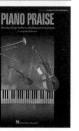